9 HABITS OF HEALTHY CHRISTIANS

JULIAN MELGOSA and ANNETTE MELGOSA

Pacific Press®
Publishing Association

Nampa, Idaho | www.pacificpress.com

Cover design by Gerald Lee Monks
Cover design resources from iStockPhoto.com | TL stock_colors | TM Cecilie_Arcurs | TR Ljupco | BL XiXinXing | BM PeopleImages | BR 511531890 | BC sjenner13
Inside design by Aaron Troia

The authors assume full responsibility for the accuracy of all facts and quotations as cited in this book.

Purchase additional copies of this book by calling toll-free 1-800-765-6955 or by visiting adventistbookcenter.com.

Library of Congress Cataloging-in-Publication Data

Names: Melgosa, Julián, author. | Melgosa, Annette, author
Title: The nine habits of healthy Christians / Julián and Annette Melgosa.
Description: Nampa, Idaho : Pacific Press Publishing Association, [2020] | Summary: "Nine lessons from Philippians on healthful Christian living"— Provided by publisher.
Identifiers: LCCN 2020043864 | ISBN 9780816367191 (paperback) | ISBN 9780816367207 (e-book edition)
Subjects: LCSH: Mental health—Religious aspects—Christianity. | Interpersonal relations—Religious aspects—Christianity. | Well-being—Religious aspects—Christianity. | Christian life—Seventh-Day Adventist authors.
Classification: LCC BT732.4 .M38 2020 | DDC 248.4—dc23
LC record available at https://lccn.loc.gov/2020043864

January 2021

Contents

Introduction

From beginning to end, the Bible appeals to us to think and behave according to godly principles and values. It is the privilege and duty of every believer to choose, nourish, and live by the principles outlined in Scripture. This book explores some of these relevant values or virtues, which we refer to as habits.

Some of these habits are internally practiced: joy, resilience, serenity, positivity, and contentment. Some are learned and nourished in connection with others: love, humility, kindness, and gratitude. All are Christlike and biblical. Scripture shows us, through admonishment and stories of people's experiences, how we may embark upon the path that will help us form these good habits and draw closer to the image of our Creator.

It is the privilege and duty of every believer to choose, nourish, and live by the principles outlined in Scripture.

Current research has repeatedly shown that incorporating these habits into our lives is highly desirable to maintain good physical and mental health. We believe that our lives in Christ involve our whole being—including our mental and emotional processes. For this reason, we outline connections between each virtue and the prevention and improvement of major mental health concerns and their symptoms. For example, joy and positivity can help neutralize depression; serenity counteracts the effects of anxiety; kindness and gratitude improve relationships; and resilience compensates for the ravages of trauma.

This book follows a self-help style to maximize its usefulness. First, we'll examine the nature of each virtue. Then we'll look at how-tos to help readers successfully adopt, practice, strengthen, and incorporate the habits into their daily living. We also believe that reflection, individually and in small groups, contributes to one's ability to adopt new habits. This is why the end of each chapter includes questions for both individuals and small groups. These questions are aimed at increasing understanding and can motivate the reader to practice these habits.

> **The hope is that these nine habits of healthy Christians may become natural to us, not because we work hard at attaining them but because we let Jesus work within us.**

The essential difference between this and other self-help books is that, while we suggest psychological techniques and strategies, we emphasize biblical content throughout the book. This is done not only to provide standards of what God wants for us but also to motivate us, to encourage us, and to provide a spiritual avenue through the grace of God by which these virtues may take place in our lives. This central, Bible-based spiritual component is what is missing in other self-help publications.

The goal is that each of us may gain intellectual insights through reading this book. But in addition, the hope is that these nine habits of healthy Christians may become natural to us, not because we work hard at attaining them but because we let Jesus work within us. With this in mind, let us claim the biblical promise that "it is God who arms me with strength and keeps my way secure" (2 Samuel 22:33).

Joy

Rejoice in the Lord always. I will say it again: Rejoice!
—Philippians 4:4

Heather spent a few years establishing herself professionally before starting a family. At thirty-five, she and her husband decided to have a child, and she soon became pregnant. She delivered a healthy baby girl. But a few days after giving birth, Heather began to feel sad and frequently tearful. She had no appetite, experienced insomnia, and felt worthless. She no longer found enjoyment in things that had previously brought her pleasure. Most devastating to her self-esteem as a new mother, she lost interest in taking care of her little girl. Her husband and mother pushed her to see a psychiatrist.

At the doctor's office, it became apparent that Heather was experiencing an abundance of negative thoughts: She felt that she had failed her daughter because she had not been allowed to give birth in a "natural" environment. Her baby did not latch during nursing, and she had to begin feeding her formula. She considered formula less healthy and saw this as another failure. Her little girl cried during the night, and she felt incapable of soothing her. Heather felt overwhelmed and alone, as her mother did not live close enough to help with the baby very often. Each negatively viewed event reinforced the thought that Heather was not a good mother. Heather succumbed to these feelings of inadequacy and felt unable to get out of bed. Caught in a repetitive cycle of thought rumination, she rehearsed over and over the things that proved that she was an unfit mother.

The doctor prescribed antidepressants to stabilize her emotions and advised that a very important part of healing would be her participation in counseling. There she would learn how to change her thoughts and build skills that would help her regain a sense of adequacy as a new mother. This, in turn, would foster a happy, contented attitude.

Jen was of similar age and had also recently given birth to a baby girl. Like Heather, she also experienced symptoms of depression after the delivery and went to see her doctor. She was also prescribed antidepressants. In Jen's case, negative thoughts did not take a firm hold because she had learned that these thoughts do not represent reality. After a number of weeks in consultation with her psychiatrist, she was able to drop the medicine and did not need an extended period of therapy. Throughout her time of treatment, Jen chose not to believe the negative thoughts that popped into her head. Instead, she reassured herself each time negative emotions presented themselves. Jen was also dealing with problems, but she recognized the power of a hopeful attitude. During this time, her husband was unemployed, but she used to say: "He is qualified and is looking for work. I know he will find something. In the meantime, he is very good with the baby and will take good care of her after I return to work." They lived far from shopping amenities, but she reasoned: "We do have a few neighbors who might help us with our shopping." When she considered her depressive symptoms, she affirmed: "These thoughts and feelings are nasty and painful, but I am taking the prescribed medication." Each time she felt overwhelmed, she reminded herself, "I know that God is with me, and He has shown me His mercy many times in the past."

> **Each time she felt overwhelmed, she reminded herself, "I know that God is with me, and He has shown me His mercy many times in the past."**

Why couldn't Heather "make" herself happy just as Jen did? What prevented Heather from seeing the positive side of her troubles? Was Jen predetermined genetically to deal successfully with adversity while Heather was naturally predestined to unhappiness?

In many similar cases, there are genetic determinants. Researchers from the University of California and the University of Missouri[1] examined studies on the long-term happiness and other traits of identical and fraternal twins. They concluded that about 50 percent of the desirable state of happiness is due to genetics, or the natural extent to which we are inclined to be joyous or despondent. They called this inclination the *set point*, and it is assumed to be fixed and stable over time. The remainder of the happiness pie, however, is divided into surrounding circumstances (10 percent) and one's own choices, decisions, and agency (40 percent). While our inherited set point, or inclination toward happiness or despondency, is real, we must also recognize that we can control a significant portion of our sense of well-being. We are told by the apostle Paul to "rejoice." Rejoicing focuses our attention on the things that we can change.

Current times seem filled with more sadness and less happiness. A recent macro-study led by Jean Twenge[2] from San Diego State University used data from more than 200,000 adolescents (ages 12–17) and almost 400,000 young adults (ages 18–25). Participants were asked to rate their distress over the past month in terms of feeling nervous, hopeless, restless, fidgety, sad, or depressed; feeling that nothing could cheer them up; feeling that everything was an effort; and feeling down on themselves, no good, or worthless. They also reported their frequency of suicidal thoughts, plans, and attempts. Figures were compared with prior records, and it was found that between 2005 and 2017, depression rates increased 52 percent in adolescents and, between 2009 and 2017, 63 percent in young adults. Rates in adults (26 and older) also increased but moderately by comparison.

Against these odds, we must make a concerted effort to become happier people. This is particularly true for Christians because we can know the joy of salvation.

First how-to: Rejoice

Joy is incompatible with depression. The states of joy and depression cannot coexist simultaneously. Paul's appeal for joy in Philippians 4:4 resonates with messages from previous paragraphs in the same letter to the Philippians: "Rejoice with me" (Philippians 2:18) and "Rejoice in the Lord" (Philippians 3:1). In Philippians 4:4, the apostle adds "always," which could be rendered as "all the time." This message invites the reader to do whatever it takes to make joy a *predominant* emotion, thus keeping depression away.

But is this a fair admonition? Are we able to rejoice at will, or are we subject to genetic traits and other circumstances outside of our control? Consider the evidence of MRI readings that show that brain activity is different when people follow instructions to worry or not to worry about something. We can conclude from this that people are, to a large extent, able to regulate their emotions. Research shows that people can learn to exercise significant control over their moods. People can learn how to adopt and maintain an attitude of happiness and act in certain uplifting ways according to personal choice. In fact, psychotherapists today spend much time teaching clients how to build positive feelings and emotions by thinking and acting intentionally in certain ways. Cognitive-behavioral therapy promotes reasonable control over mood toward attaining joy and happiness.

Rejoicing focuses our attention on the things that we can change.

Sonja Lyubomirsky, director of the Postive Activities and Well-Being Laboratory in Riverside, at the University of California, Riverside, is a leading figure in positive psychology. She and her team conduct research to identify behaviors and attitudes that help people experience happier moods. Paul was not being unreasonable when he urged his readers to rejoice. To improve your state of joy, try the following activities based on Lyubomirsky's recommendations:[3]

- Express gratitude. Write a letter of appreciation, make a phone call, or pay a visit to thank someone for something specific that they have done for you. These simple acts can bring positive change. Experimental studies reveal that men and women who offer appreciation, no matter their age or health, feel better than those who *receive* it, just as Jesus Himself affirmed (Acts 20:35).

- Practice optimism. Optimism is very desirable and can lead to a stable sense of well-being. Optimism is not illusory or unable to recognize drawbacks. Rather, it focuses on the bright side of things while trying to repair what is wrong. Perhaps that is why it is said that a pessimist sees difficulty in every opportunity, while an optimist sees opportunity in every difficulty.

- Avoid overthinking. A worrisome thought, when rehearsed again and again, is like someone trying to go to sleep in a state of alertness—tossing over and over to no avail. You must break the cycle. How? Psychologists teach patients to distract themselves by changing activity (for example, calling someone or working out). If a problem is real, instead of worrying, jot down possible solutions. If there seems to be no solution, identify healthier ways (other than worry) to respond to the problem. Ask someone to help you. Then start trying the solutions.

- Practice random acts of kindness. It is well known that someone who is discouraged or affected by depression can feel better by helping someone else in need. Consider helping someone to be a way of following in the steps of Jesus, who "went around doing good and healing all who were under the power of the devil" (Acts 10:38).

- Forgive. Extending forgiveness is a key factor in happiness. Experts recommend it, and not necessarily for moral reasons. However, when forgiveness is guided by moral principles, it becomes more authentic and complete because then forgiveness is granted wholly, unconditionally, and out of the love that comes as a gift from God.

- Savor the small things. Expensive or impressive pastimes do not lead to joy. Rather, learn to observe and enjoy the simple things in life: a natural landscape, a good friend, a great book or piece of music, prayers of thanksgiving, a simple meal, or a relaxing walk. All of these activities can improve your mood.

- Practice the religious life. Contemporary psychology recognizes the health benefits of religion, and the American Psychological Association now has the Division of Religion and Spirituality. Prayer, churchgoing, outreach, reading of sacred texts, and fellowship with other believers have been studied empirically and found to foster well-being.

- Nourish relationships. Connecting with others improves your mood. Sharing good news can be a source of happiness. In the parable of the lost coin, the Bible explains: "And when she finds it, she calls her friends and neighbors together and says, '*Rejoice* with me' " (Luke 15:9; emphasis added).

- Find and practice your personal strengths and virtues. The happiest people are those who understand their strengths (such as persistence, ability to communicate, or logical reasoning) and virtues (such as compassion, fairness, authenticity, or humility) and how to use them to benefit others. This brings to mind the gifts of the Spirit referred to in 1 Corinthians 12. These gifts are a path to well-being and allow us to better serve God and others.

The concepts just listed are proven to increase joy and happiness. But there is a further step. The apostle says, "Rejoice *in the Lord*." This adds the most important dimension. Psychological techniques and strategies are helpful in lifting your mood, but the Lord can strengthen and complete your happiness, making it permanent. Rejoicing "in the Lord" means surrendering to Him, accepting His gift of salvation, and experiencing the fullness of gratitude. It means believing that His love is so immense that it communicates joy. Experiencing His presence in our lives each day makes us happy enough that we will share our joy with those around us. This is authentic happiness.

> **Rejoicing "in the Lord" means surrendering to Him, accepting His gift of salvation, and experiencing the fullness of gratitude.**

Second how-to: Keep busy

Jesus did and said so many things that "if every one of them were written down, I suppose that even the whole world would not have room for the books that would be written" (John 21:25). It is difficult to imagine Him in idleness. We are told that "each day Jesus was teaching at the temple, and each evening he went out to spend the night on the hill called the Mount of Olives, and all the people came early in the morning to hear him at the temple" (Luke 21:37, 38). He also healed the sick until there was no more illness in a town:

Hour after hour they came and went. . . .
Not until the last sufferer had been relieved did Jesus cease His work.[4]

Joy

Keeping yourself busy is not just a matter of accomplishing more things; it also protects against mental maladies and promotes a happy mood. To keep yourself busy and motivated, try the following:

- Set goals for yourself. Whether it is a do-it-yourself project, visiting someone, or completing an entire degree, you must be clear about what you want to accomplish. Be realistic—setting too many goals and not accomplishing them is disappointing; on the other hand, goals that are too small may not motivate and satisfy you.

- Don't be perfectionistic. This may lead to spending too much time planning rather than doing and may also lead to countless "barriers" and "errors" that will prevent you from advancing. To counteract this, impose time limits (*I must finish this by four o'clock!*).

- Find social support. Although many things may be performed individually, when you carry out a project with someone else, it is easier to keep at it and avoid discouragement. In choosing a work partner, find someone who is positive, thus avoiding unnecessary negativity.

- Take the first step and start. The simple act of beginning might provide the necessary push to take you to the next step and onward. Writers know that when they lack inspiration, they must push themselves to write anyway. Even if the result is poor, it can be corrected and improved. It is always easier to work with something than with nothing.

- Keep physically active. An active lifestyle provides extensive benefits to both physical and mental health. The link between exercise and good mood is indisputable. People being treated for depression, anxiety, bipolar disorder, and other serious mental conditions are routinely assigned physical activities, preferably in the company of others.

- Get involved in learning. Education, as evidenced by research, is the single variable most strongly associated with health and longevity. Of course, living a healthy, long life is a solid foundation for happiness. Learning does not need to involve a formal degree at a prestigious university. Explore courses at a community college or a local foundation. Or find ways to regularly seek out information. Read about particular topics of interest. Any of these activities transmit the joy of learning, which is a long-lasting emotion.

Third how-to: Focus on happiness and contentment

Some teach that one should not focus on the past because the future is what really counts. Others say that contemplating the past helps avoid future problems and helps us attain our goals. Still others say that we possess neither the past nor the future—only the present, and our emphasis should therefore be on the here and now. All of these perspectives are true but incomplete. It is better to look at the past, the present, and the future positively. It is healthy to remember the good of the past and learn from the old mistakes, to experience the present with joy and enthusiasm, and to look toward the future with anticipation and hope.

- Follow happy people. One method consists of identifying happy people and finding out about their habits and lifestyle. Start with their relationships. Happy people are good at relationships in general: family, friends, colleagues, even pets! Next, explore and emulate how they view life. They are likely grateful and helpful, optimistic about the future, and committed to their life goals. Many are also spiritual or religious.

- Adhere to and grow positive psychology principles. Positive psychology founder Martin Seligman summarizes the principal components of this field with the acronym PERMA, which stands for positive emotions, engagement, relationships, meaning, and achievement.[5] Review each of these and incorporate them into your daily life:

    ○ Positive emotions—joy, love, serenity, compassion, gratitude, hope, confidence, or contentment

    ○ Engagement—intense involvement in a preferred activity to the point of losing track of time

Joy

- Relationships—optimal connection with others

- Meaning—the ability to see significance and purpose in life events; for the believer, this means acknowledging that God is directing things in one's life and in the world

- Achievement—setting and envisioning goals, creating action plans, moving toward them, and reframing obstacles to see them as challenges

Joy counts among the highest blessings and can be adopted and nourished. According to Paul, Christians should seek joy. Jesus experienced many emotions, including joy. He shared joy with His disciples "so that they may have the full measure of my joy within them" (John 17:13). Jesus wants all of His followers to experience joy. Use the tools available to you and, above all, partner with Jesus and ask Him to put His joy within you.

Reflection questions and activities for individuals

1. Choose two or three ideas from this chapter that may fit your personality and lifestyle. Plan to apply them over the next few days. Ask God to bless your effort to become a happier Christian. Note any changes in your mood as a result of the practice.

_____

_____

_____

_____

2. To exercise your ability to think positively, reflect on an adverse episode from your past. Naturally, there were many negative aspects to it. However, in perspective, can you also think of something good that came from it?

_____

_____

_____

_____

_____

3. List two or three personal strengths or virtues that you possess. Think of how you might use these to benefit someone in need. Then follow through and observe how serving others affects your mood.

_____

_____

_____

_____

4. Keeping busy is one of the best ways to promote happiness and prevent depression. What can you do to fill idle time? Find wholesome ways to complete your activities, thus avoiding the negative thoughts surrounding unfinished work.

_____

_____

_____

_____

5. Review your social interactions. Do you have too many or too few? Do those people with whom you associate transmit joy, or do they tend to be negativistic or depressing? Identify what you can do to build positive relationships.

_____

_____

_____

_____

6. Determine how you can incorporate antidepression measures into your life, such as expressing gratitude, engaging in physical exercise, or granting forgiveness.

_____

_____

_____

_____

_____

Joy

Discussion questions and activities for small groups

1. Discuss with your group the influence of heredity and environment on people's ability to experience happiness. How can choice and determination help? How can our relationship with God make a radical difference?

2. Share with your group your reflection on the verse, "Those who are kind benefit themselves" (Proverbs 11:17). How do you think this happens? Consider organizing a group project to show kindness.

3. Share with your group one or two things that make you happy. Share also one or two religious or spiritual activities that bring joy to your life.

4. Read John 17:13. Why is Jesus praying specifically for His disciples to have joy? What would promote (or impede) the fulfillment of Jesus' prayer?

5. Share a time when you expressed specific gratitude to someone and how you felt afterward.

6. Share a time when you granted forgiveness to someone. How did it make you feel?

---

1. Sonja Lyubomirsky, Kennon M. Sheldon, and David Schkade, "Pursuing Happiness: The Architecture of Sustainable Change," *Review of General Psychology* 9, no. 2 (2005): 111–131.

2. Jean M. Twenge et. al, "Age, Period, and Cohort Trends in Mood Disorder Indicators and Suicide-Related Outcomes in a Nationally Representative Dataset, 2005–2017," *Journal of Abnormal Psychology* 128, no. 3, (2019): 185–199, https://dx.doi.org/10.1037/abn0000410.

3. Lyubomirsky, Sheldon, and Schkade, "Pursuing Happiness," 111–131.

4. Ellen G. White, *The Desire of Ages* (Nampa, ID: Pacific Press®, 2005), 259.

5. Martin Seligman, "PERMA™ Theory of Well-Being and PERMA™ Workshops," Positive Psychology Center, accessed September 29, 2020, https://ppc.sas.upenn.edu/learn-more/perma-theory-well-being-and-perma-workshops.

Love

*My brothers and sisters, you whom I love
and long for, my joy and crown.*

—Philippians 4:1

Most joy, as well as pain, comes to us through social connections. When we ask participants in our seminars to share personal examples of rewarding, fulfilling, nourishing, and enjoyable experiences, most involve the company of others. This is also true when we ask them to think of situations that caused them embarrassment, discomfort, or frustration. Successful interactions with people are one of the greatest sources of support, bringing great joy, excitement, and happiness. But too often, personal interaction also brings distress, anger, and disappointment.

Although social connections can be problematic, most people seek the company of others. In fact, when people find themselves alone, they look for social substitutions to compensate for the lack of human presence. They engage in what psychologists call social snacking—a pseudo-social encounter. Social snacking mimics genuine human interaction, according to Peter Jonason and his colleagues,[1] who studied 306 participants, ages eighteen to sixty-five, at New Mexico University. Behaviors included self-talk, singing to oneself, talking to pets as to humans, or turning on the TV.

Social snacking behaviors, such as using TV as a social substitute, provide vocal and visual signals that a person perceives similarly to real social interaction. This partially meets our need for social interaction.

Since human interaction is so important to our lives, every effort to nourish relationships is worth making. Counseling services offer help for many types of relationships: couples, peers, friends, neighbors, associates, and relatives, to name a few. Sometimes, corporations invest in workshops and other events designed to promote more peaceful relationships between coworkers and across levels of the hierarchy. They know that smooth interactions bring not only personal and group well-being but also higher efficacy.

The Bible is rich in principles and guidelines to help us build good relationships within the Christian context.

For the follower of Jesus, nourishing interpersonal connections transcends business goals or better mental health. It is a mandate to practice the very essence of God's nature—love. The Bible is rich in principles and guidelines to help us build good relationships within the Christian context. Relying on biblical principles and applying the advice of specialists within the parameters of biblical guidance, let me present five pieces of advice, or how-tos.

First how-to: Use affectionate language

Kind words, spoken sincerely, can set a positive emotional tone. In his letter to the church in Philippi, Paul uses this type of communication before addressing an interpersonal issue that was taking place in the church: "Therefore, my brothers and sisters, you whom I love and long for, my joy and crown, stand firm in the Lord in this way, dear friends" (Philippians 4:1).

Paul is able to address the church in a warm and intimate way, using only one beautiful sentence! He addresses the readers as family—brothers and sisters. He expresses clear affection—"I love you, I long for you"—and manifests how precious they are to him, describing them as his crown. Other versions use terms such as "beloved," "dear friends," "most desired," (DRA) "you bring me joy and make me proud of you" (ERV), or "how happy you make me" (GNT).

Expressions of affection using clear and direct verbal and nonverbal forms not only increase mutual satisfaction but also strengthen commitment within relationships. The apostle is applying this psychological principle as he verbalizes appreciation for his audience. Many people have trouble expressing this kind of language and emotional tone. Why don't we use this type of language more often? Why do we hesitate to express gratitude and fondness?

There are several reasons: culture, personality, or a hectic lifestyle all play a role. But there is one additional reason that psychologists have identified: a poor self-concept. People with low self-esteem (self-respect) are inclined to offer less-affectionate messages. On the other hand, those with a balanced view of their abilities tend to show warmth naturally, which adds quality to the relationship and a greater sense of well-being.

Psychologists and counselors try to help patients focus on their own strengths to help raise their self-worth. But, as believers, we have a less self-centered way available to us. We seek to adjust the way we see ourselves, and most importantly, we focus on *who* God created us to be and how God *sees* us, as revealed in Scripture. Take, for example, the following texts:

- "I praise you because I am fearfully and wonderfully made" (Psalm 139:14).

- "He chose us in him before the creation of the world" (Ephesians 1:4).

- "I have called you friends" (John 15:15).

- "You were redeemed . . . with the precious blood of Christ" (1 Peter 1:18, 19).

- "You made [humankind] a little lower than the angels" (Hebrews 2:7).

Becoming familiar with these passages can bring extraordinary blessings. Try to commit these and similar texts to memory or carry them written on a card. Repeat them frequently. Consider the way God *sees* you, not the way others evaluate you.

Second how-to: Empathize

Perhaps you've heard this story by an unknown author. One day, a farmer posted a sign out by his driveway advertising puppies for sale. He heard a boy's voice behind him. The boy asked, "Sir, how much is one of those puppies?" The farmer explained that these puppies came from fine parents and grandparents and that they were expensive. The boy searched his pockets and came up with $7.50. The man was touched and felt that this boy deserved a puppy. He called for the mother dog, Callie, who came running, followed by five lively little bundles of fur. An instant later, another, noticeably smaller, lame puppy emerged from the doghouse and courageously tried to catch up with his siblings. "That's the one!" the boy said excitedly. To this, the farmer said, "Sonny, I don't think he would be able to play and run with you as these other puppies would

The point here was not to take sides on an issue but to repair a relationship.

. . ." The boy rolled up one of his pants legs to reveal a steel brace running down his leg. He explained: "You see, I don't run well myself, and I think that little puppy needs someone who understands."

Empathy is the ability to feel another's emotions. It is highly desirable because it brings psychological well-being, helps us feel loved and accepted by others, prevents and resolves conflicts, promotes altruism, and exemplifies a deeper way to live the Christian life.

Apparently, the sisters Euodia and Syntyche in the New Testament church of Philippi were not behaving with empathy toward each other. Paul asked them to try to understand each other: "I plead with Euodia and I plead with Syntyche to be of the same mind in the Lord" (Philippians 4:2). Notice the repetition of the active verb: "I *plead with* Euodia and I *plead with* Syntyche." This was grammatically unnecessary, and it could be considered repetitive. However, Paul did not want to convey the idea that he favored one or the other. Instead, he presented his plea to each sister equally. The point here was not to take sides on an issue but to repair a relationship.

How might we develop empathy? Like any habit, we learn through practice. The more we practice, the better we become, until we master the skill and it becomes part of us. Try the following strategies to practice empathy:

- Listen attentively when people speak to you. This means that you make an intentional effort to understand—you look at their faces and avoid the automatic tendency to tune them out while you think of how you will respond.

- Reflect on the experiences of others when you hear or read about them; this is especially helpful when it involves those who are different from you. Consider ethnic or socioeconomic groups who are different from you, including those less fortunate and those who have greater advantages than you.

- Physically accompany and observe someone as the person works through a task; this may involve a task at work or home. This technique is especially helpful for building empathy if the tasks you pick are unfamiliar or difficult for you.

Third how-to: Don't play the power game

The actual dispute between Euodia and Syntyche is not recorded in Scripture. However, it must have been of relevance to the entire community, for their names are mentioned in a public letter to the church. Perhaps the problem had to do with a power struggle—one of the most common reasons for conflict.

Too many times, interpersonal difficulties arise because people place themselves higher than others! Social psychology has long suggested that there are two basic positions in relationships: dominance and submissiveness. The dominant side is referred to as *the one-up*; the submissive is called *the one-down*. When the power hierarchy is well understood and accepted, roles are complementary and conflict is rare.

Our family lived in Southeast Asia for almost a decade. There we learned that hierarchy is very important. Everyone clearly understands who is above and who is beneath. This is easily observed when greeting a relative. Take, for example, a son-in-law and a mother-in-law in Thailand. To greet each other, both use the *wai*—a slight bow, with palms pressed together in a prayer-like manner. If one observes carefully, the son-in-law positions his hands higher than his mother-in-law and bows lower than she does. This means that he is showing her respect. This style of greeting happens not only between family members but also at work, in business, and in any setting where greetings occur. Someone may look at this as a rigid way to perpetuate differences and preserve power. However, practices like these prevent much conflict and embarrassment.

While proper understanding and acceptance of social norms allow us to live harmoniously within established societal hierarchies and can help smooth human relationships, there is a better biblical way: humility. This virtue is not to be confused with unhealthy submission to abuse. True humility works best when practiced by both parties and is the appropriate response when there is discord in interpersonal interactions. Appeals to humility abound in Psalms, Proverbs, the Gospels, and in the Pauline letters. Humility is one of the most exalted virtues in the Bible. God asks us to exercise humility, for He knows how this will improve relationships. Often, humility freely given by one party allows the other to do the same. Many problems would disappear if both parties in a dispute followed counsel such as the following:

- "Learn from me, for I am gentle and humble in heart" (Matthew 11:29).

- "Be completely humble and gentle; be patient, bearing with one another in love" (Ephesians 4:2).

- "Submit to one another out of reverence for Christ" (Ephesians 5:21).

- "In humility value others above yourselves" (Philippians 2:3).

- "My heart is not proud, Lord, my eyes are not haughty" (Psalm 131:1).

- "Before a downfall the heart is haughty, but humility comes before honor" (Proverbs 18:12).

How do you cultivate humility in your daily habits? The answer is to strengthen your relationship with Jesus through regularly praying, reading His story, and reflecting on His words and actions. As you grow closer to Christ, you will grow in all of His attributes, including humility. In addition, here are some practical ways to exercise humility:

- Express gratitude. Gratitude and humility go hand in hand. Tell a friend, a colleague, or a member of your family how grateful you are for something specific that person has done. Say it orally or through a written note, and say it frequently. When you say, "Thank you," add why you are thankful, briefly and directly.

- Speak less of yourself. Ask: "Can I reduce the amount of self-reporting and be more attentive to what others tell me?" If the answer is yes, make an extra effort to focus on what you are hearing. Understanding other people will make you humbler. As Rick Warren wrote, "Humility is not thinking less of yourself; it is thinking of yourself less."[2]

- Do not interfere in the affairs of others unless asked. By interjecting your views, you place yourself in a position of superiority ("I know better, this is how you should do it . . ."). This is a barrier to humility.

- Accept and recognize your mistakes and errors. This may be hard, but with prayer and practice, it will become a habit. Also, admit when you do not know something.

- Seek advice when necessary. Remember that you have limitations and that you will benefit from the help and support of others. This may feel like weakness, but it is not.

Fourth how-to: Practice forgiveness and reconciliation

In the past, forgiveness was viewed as a spiritual discipline rather than a health benefit, and those who didn't feel the need to render account to God could hold a grudge seemingly without consequence. Today, forgiveness is "prescribed" by mental health practitioners to believers and nonbelievers alike to alleviate anxiety, stress, hostility, high blood pressure, and depression and to strengthen the immune system. Its beneficial effect at freeing a person from feelings of resentment is now recognized.

Holding a grudge imprisons you, but forgiveness sets you free.

Many interpersonal conflicts are rooted in offenses where the refusal to forgive subsequently led to significant unhappiness. That is why forgiveness is so important and why today it is recommended that a person do whatever it takes to accomplish it. For the believer, this means depending on God to grant forgiveness to the offender no matter the intention or the size of the offense.

In addition to the moral damage that an unwillingness to forgive causes, it also results in loss of freedom. Lewis Smedes, the author of a seminal book on forgiveness, *Forgive and Forget*, wrote that to forgive is to "set a prisoner free [and] discover that the real prisoner was yourself."[3] Holding a grudge imprisons you, but forgiveness sets you free.

Reconciliation is a step beyond forgiveness. Sometimes, forgiveness can occur without the need for reconciliation. When Marcos opened and stepped through a door into a government building, he did not expect the employee on the other side to rudely accuse him of using the wrong door and to belittle him. Marcos was understandably upset. After all, there was no sign on the door saying not to enter. Also, he was on his way to complete a transaction in that office. Marcos couldn't shake his resentment. He mentally rehearsed acts of retaliation. He decided to pray about it and afterward felt better. Then, in his mind, he forgave the civil servant, and this allowed him to consider the circumstance from her perspective. In other words, he began to be empathetic. Perhaps she was having a bad day or was feeling angry about something else. Once he could react empathetically, Marcos was able to dismiss the event and move on to other things in his day. In this case, there was no need for reconciliation—the civil servant probably didn't know that she had hurt Marcos, and they did not need to see each other again. Marcos let go of his resentment and closed that event in his life.

> **Reconciliation, on the other hand, is practiced when people wish to restore a relationship.**

Reconciliation, on the other hand, is practiced when people wish to restore a relationship. While forgiveness may or may not need the participation of the offender, reconciliation always does. In words often attributed to Lewis Smedes, "It takes one person to forgive, it takes two people to be reunited." Jesus counseled, "Leave your gift there in front of the altar. First go and *be reconciled* to them; then come and offer your gift" (Matthew 5:24; emphasis added). Reconciliation is an interpersonal process where you dialog with the offender about what happened, exchange caring comments about the hurt that was inflicted, listen attentively, and begin to rebuild trust.

Fifth how-to: Use mediation if necessary

Returning to the dispute between sisters Euodia and Syntyche, Paul writes to the principal reader of his letter: "I ask you, my true companion, help these women" (Philippians

Love

4:3). This unnamed individual was to serve as an instrument of reconciliation.

One of the fastest-growing areas within the behavioral sciences is industrial/organizational (I/O) psychology. I/O psychologists work with individuals and groups inside corporations. They study the dynamics of the workplace. They promote the well-being of employees and help enhance their performance. They also apply psychological principles to solve interpersonal conflict—one of the most common sources of stress in organizations. Often, these psychologists play the role of mediators, just as Paul asks of his "true companion."

But why do people fall into conflict? Sometimes, it is because of the power struggle growing out of one feeling stronger than the other. It may also occur when the resources (money, space, privileges, and so on) are limited and each party believes he or she deserves them more than others; or there may be differences in values or beliefs, and people haven't learned tolerance. Finally, there may not be actual reasons for conflict, but the involved individuals have distorted perceptions that lead to misunderstandings.

When people are caught in the middle of these difficulties, many become emotionally charged, unable to reason, and incapable of resolving the conflict. Their assessment of the situation is so individualistic that they have great difficulty in seeing the other's perspective.

In those circumstances, the role of a mediator may prove useful. A mediator will typically act as a go-between, assisting two people or groups in coming together in mutual understanding. The mediator must be impartial, objective, and fair. He or she must not take sides or use threats or manipulation. Mediators also train people to use several strategies:

- Listen honestly in order to better understand the problem.

- Steer clear of manipulation, threats, or intimidation.

- Focus on the problem, not on the person.

- Use *I* messages and avoid *you* messages to prevent putting the blame on others.

- Approach *the process* of handling the conflict with care—if the process is perceived as fair, a resolution is more likely.

- Seek to assign due responsibility to each side.

- Focus on the future and put the past aside.

- Seek a win-win solution.

- Forgive—a crucial stage to achieve well-being and to face the future with hope.

To close this chapter, consider for a moment a group of animals coexisting in the forest. The most powerful animal is the bear. It does not have natural predators. Other animals in the forest know this and do not challenge bears. These powerful animals are the supreme beasts in their environment. But sometimes they must learn to coexist with others, like the skunk, to avoid the unpleasant consequence that comes from disturbing these weaker creatures. There have been reports of a grizzly bear allowing his food to be eaten by a skunk.

In the family, at church, at work, or at school, we are all part of the same team and need to learn to coexist with one another. Remember the valuable Scripture texts that can help us enhance our interpersonal relationships. In your prayer life, ask for wisdom to apply these principles to all your interpersonal and social interactions.

Reflection questions and activities for individuals

1. When do you use warm and affectionate language? With whom? How can you add affirming, caring, and warmhearted statements to your normal speech?

   _____

   _____

   _____

   _____

2. How might you better learn about and understand other people's situations? What might you do specifically to improve your empathy toward them?

   _____

   _____

   _____

Love

3. How might an attitude of humility assist you in resolving a problem with someone else?

_____

_____

_____

4. Reflect on problems, issues, or conflicts at work and at home. What might you do to resolve them following biblical principles?

_____

_____

_____

_____

5. If you were asked to act as a mediator with fellow workers, students, or church members, what basic principles would you follow when meeting with those in conflict?

_____

_____

_____

_____

6. Is there anyone in your life you need to forgive or with whom you need to reconcile? Draw up a plan based on the biblical principles outlined in this chapter and pray for God's power to carry it out.

_____

_____

_____

_____

Discussion questions and activities for small groups

1. How do you react to someone who uses loving and caring statements? To those who respond in anger or with rudeness? What is the Christian way to deal with both types of situations? Share your thoughts with your group.

2. If Euodia and Syntyche were members of your community, what would likely be topics of conflict? In your group, discuss scenarios and propose solutions.

3. What sort of interpersonal issues typically arise in your communities, families, or groups of friends? What would be the Christian way to resolve these?

4. As a group, discuss ways that the smartphone is altering how people relate to one another. How might a smartphone be used to strengthen human ties? Name some uses that weaken these ties.

5. Share with the members of your group examples of two people for whom you are especially grateful and state why. Commit publicly to express openly, clearly, and directly your gratitude to these individuals.

6. What do you consider to be the most important quality of a mediator or a peace-maker? Ask each member of your group and compare responses.

---

1. Peter K. Jonason, Gregory D. Webster, and A. Elizabeth Lindsey, "Solutions to the Problem of Diminished Social Interaction," *Evolutionary Psychology* 6, no. 4 (October 2008): 637–651, https://doi.org/10.1177/147470490800600410.

2. Rick Warren, *The Purpose Driven Life* (Grand Rapids, MI: Zondervan, 2002), 148.

3. Lewis B. Smedes, *Forgive and Forget: Healing the Hurts We Don't Deserve* (New York: HarperCollins, 1984), 133.

Resilience

What has happened to me has actually served to advance the gospel.
—Philippians 1:12

One of the most moving contemporary stories of resilience is that of Mende Nazer, a twelve-year-old girl from Sudan whose village was raided by a ring of human traffickers in the midst of the Sudanese Civil War in 1994. As she attempted to flee with her family up the mountains in the Nuba region, family members became separated in the commotion. Mende was captured and added to some thirty other abducted children and adolescents. She was raped by her captors and then taken to Sudan's capital city, Khartoum, where she was sold to a family, forced to work, and repeatedly abused physically. After enduring this treatment for more than six years, Mende was sent to serve the family of a Sudan embassy employee in Willesden, northwest London. While running an errand and with the help of a Sudanese man she accidentally met, Mende escaped from slavery.

In spite of her ordeals, Mende gained sufficient courage and strength to attempt to normalize her life. Once free, Mende sought political asylum in the UK and was denied. Rather than giving up, she became active in discussing issues of contemporary slavery and writing about her experiences. Mende was finally granted asylum and, eventually, citizenship. Her next goal was to reconnect with her family in Sudan, which she managed to do. Mende married a former refugee man, also from Sudan, and she is now part of her own foundation that provides education and water to her people in the Nuba Mountains.

Nine Habits of Healthy Christians

What was the secret that allowed Mende to survive so many years of torment? How did she develop resilience? Mende talks about her faith in God and her hope and determination to see her family again. Mende published her entire story in the book *Slave*, in which she tells about her childhood at home, her life as a slave both in Khartoum and London, and her escape and eventual asylum.

Although pain and suffering were never part of God's original plan for humankind, terrible things happen to people, causing much pain and trauma. Regardless of how terrible events may be, a person can, with time and effort, develop resilience.

Regardless of how terrible events may be, a person can, with time and effort, develop resilience.

Resilience (or resiliency) is a concept originally linked to industry. Engineers refer to resilience as the ability that materials possess to return to their original condition after having stress applied to them. Psychology borrowed the concept to explain how people, when submitted to stress and adversity, may recover, "bounce back," and become stronger. This has been found to be true among single mothers with small children, those living in extreme poverty, people diagnosed with terminal illnesses and their loved ones, whole families who lose their jobs, individuals involved in severe accidents, women and other family members who have been abused, displaced people, refugees, incarcerated men and women, and others. Many succumb under such pressure, but others seem capable of enduring suffering and growing from it.

The Bible is rich in stories of individuals who demonstrated this desirable trait. In fact, it seems like Bible stories present more people under tribulation who rise to victory than not. And through their lives, we learn that the ability to bounce back comes from God. Take Moses, for example. We know very little about his life at the pharaoh's palace, but from the time he awoke to the condition of his people and decided to lead them to freedom, he repeatedly faced persecution and rejection, not only from the oppressive Egyptians but also from the very people God liberated through him. Yet, he lived a life of communion with God, accomplished great things for his people and for the Lord's glory, and in the end, "he did not regret the burdens he had borne."[1] He lived to be 120 years old and had normal eyesight and physical strength to the end of his life (Deuteronomy 34:7).

Another example of resilience is Paul. Highly educated and part of the ruling class, he accepted Jesus and suffered endless harassment. He offered a summary in 2 Corinthians 6:4–10 that included beatings, imprisonments, riots, hard work, sleepless nights, hunger, dishonor, sorrow—yet, with all of his losses, he considered himself as "possessing everything" (verse 10). When he was a prisoner in Rome, appearing to the casual observer as a loser, he saw his condition with a purpose: "What has happened to me has actually served to advance the gospel" (Philippians 1:12). He could have chosen to be discontent, to feel sorry for himself and repeatedly ask God why He allowed these things to happen. He could have also argued that he would be more useful if he were freed and able to visit churches and to preach the gospel wherever needed.

One secret of resiliency is understanding that God has a specific plan for each situation, even those that are painful and without apparent sense. In addition, one needs to believe that God is always ready to provide the necessary support at the right time. These thoughts will prevent despair and promote hope. Moses and Paul are just two examples of resilient people in the Bible. Rich stories of adversity run through the lives of Job, Noah, Abraham, Jacob, Joseph, Gideon, Joshua, Caleb, Naomi, David, Daniel, Esther, Nehemiah, Stephen, Peter, Timothy, and, of course, Jesus, who was subjected to the most extreme pressure and overcame evil and sin forever.

I believe that religious hope and faith are key factors in resilience. It is true that many nonbelievers are champions of resilience, but it is truer that those who believe in a loving and gracious Savior have hope and certainty of temporal relief as well as eternal salvation. Mende's case reminds us of these two foundational features in survival and bouncing back: faith in God and hope that things will become better.

A study conducted at the University of Birmingham in the United Kingdom[2] was done by means of in-depth, semi-structured interviews with a group of participants. Most had left their country of origin and were refugees or asylum seekers. They had experienced abandoning their country due to war or persecution and adapting to a new culture. Some people think that arriving in a wealthy society from a place of poverty or persecution must be, by contrast, pleasant. But it is not so, at least not for a significant period of time. One may be surrounded by comfort and opportunities, but those things are perceived as painful because they belong to others. In addition, newcomers feel that they do not belong and tend to experience constant fear of being rejected or deported.

The study showed that those who found support in religion and spirituality were better able to increase resilience than those who were not believers. Namely, those using religious coping skills improved in three specific areas: adjusting to the host country, dealing with parting and separation, and facing issues of discrimination and exclusion.

The difference between a person with faith and one without is encapsulated in the ongoing divine intervention and obedience on the part of the affected—"for though the righteous fall seven times, they rise again, but the wicked stumble when calamity strikes" (Proverbs 24:16). How can we achieve resilience in practical ways? The how-tos that follow offer strategies that can support us when we experience pain and can help us bounce back with more strength in the end.

First how-to: Prayer

Even if you cannot understand your circumstances and are overwhelmed in the middle of adversity, seek God in prayer. Job did it in the middle of his suffering and confusion: "God's voice thunders in marvelous ways; he does great things beyond our understanding" (Job 37:5). Ultimately, Job was vindicated before his friends, and God restored his circumstances and allowed him to live a long and full life until he died at 140 years old. Elijah also experienced pain, perplexity, and fear. He suffered from various depressive symptoms and manifested such a deep desire to die that he asked God to take his life. The story tells us that in spite of his desperate prayer, he was healed and was allowed to anoint the next king and the next prophet. He also received the comforting news that seven thousand in Israel had not bowed down or worshiped Baal (1 Kings 19:18). Lastly, he was taken to heaven in a fiery chariot instead of experiencing death (2 Kings 2:11).

Yes, if you are as confused and desperate as Job or as depressed as Elijah, offer a prayer;

approach God in your pain, and He will listen. It is better to offer Elijah's prayer of hopelessness than no prayer at all. And if, in your fragile emotional state, you cannot pray, ask a close friend to pray for you.

Reading the Bible may also bring your mind closer to God. You may find that reading takes effort in moments of difficulty. If so, try listening to an audio version of the Bible or uplifting music. These approaches will move you in the right direction to endure adversity and to come out stronger in the end.

Second how-to: Use coping strategies

Counselors, psychologists, social workers, and other mental health professionals recommend resilience strategies that can be used successfully by Christians. These have worked well in clinical settings, and many have been confirmed by empirical research. When combined with trust in God, they become especially powerful. If you are being tested in some aspect of your life or simply wish to acquire habits to protect your mental and emotional health, try these and see whether you experience strength and look toward the future with hope:

> Yes, if you are as confused and desperate as Job or as depressed as Elijah, offer a prayer; approach God in your pain, and He will listen.

- Remember events from your past when you experienced turmoil, but with necessary time and actions, your pain came to an end, and your emotions returned to a state of calmness.

- Practice an enjoyable hobby where you can keep your mind and/or body active. This will help you stop focusing on pain and suffering by directing your mind elsewhere until the storm passes.

- Listen to music. Choose a type of music that soothes your spirit and improves your mood.

- Seek moments of solitude as well as times of positive and soothing social interaction. Both are necessary as only one tends to be insufficient.

- Change activities with relative frequency to prevent your mind from settling into rumination.

- Learn to savor the small things of life. For example, observe children's play, listen to soft music, visit a friend, enjoy a simple meal, witness a sunrise or sunset.

- Find moments of wonder in nature to contemplate things like a sunrise, a sunset, or an ample landscape.

- Write. Put some of your grateful thoughts in writing, along with your frustrations and perplexities. You may also write out a prayer.

Third how-to: Exchange support

Many consider it a weakness to need support. Others believe that if they receive help, they must reciprocate, which may make them reluctant to accept help. But healthy human interaction calls for exchange, and very specifically, Jesus reminds us that "it is more blessed to give than to receive" (Acts 20:35).

Therefore, when you are experiencing trouble and someone offers help, accept it graciously. And in any case, be proactive in offering your help and support to others. These are some suggestions on how to do it:

- Ask a friend to help you with something practical. Whether it is running an errand or giving you a hand with the house or the children in a hectic situation, go and ask kindly. A good friend will feel honored to be asked and will be happy to help.

- Do something for someone. Explore the possible needs of your friend, neighbor, or relative and offer specific ways you can help. You may need to offer more than once.

- Donate items. You probably have too many things at home that are of little use to you and could fulfill someone else's need. Give quality things to your local community center, Goodwill, or Salvation Army, and feel good knowing that your gift may make life easier for someone.

- Donate blood occasionally. It is comforting to think that part of you may save someone's life.

- Volunteer. There are many options for you to offer your expertise and labor for free. Here are a few ideas: schools, food banks, local parks or beaches, homeless shelters, retirement homes, or animal shelters.

- Be kind and friendly. As you go places and do business, perform courteous acts, smile when appropriate, and send polite messages showing respect for others: "You go first." "Thank you." "You have been very helpful."

- Listen to someone with your mind and heart. Listening is a ministry that can be very valuable to those in pain. Try to learn about their situation and how they are feeling, and confirm openly your confidentiality. Purpose not to talk about yourself, your story, your experience, and your advice (unless asked). James knew about this human inclination: "Be quick to listen, slow to speak and slow to become angry" (James 1:19).

- Say only the right things. Paul knew about the tendency to talk improperly: "Do not let any unwholesome talk come out of your mouths, but only what is helpful for building others up according to their needs" (Ephesians 4:29).

Fourth how-to: Put things in perspective

Many people wish to live their life as if it were the script of a happily-ever-after film. Others are more fearful or negative and anticipate the worst possible outcomes. But at the end of the day, most even out—the awful expectations become much less so, and the rosy view comes with inconveniences. Knowing this, you need to look at things in perspective. These are a few suggestions to help you do it:

- When you face difficulties or experience losses, learn to think months or years ahead. What difference will this make a year from now? You will soon realize that the current disturbance or worry often vanishes when seen in the long term.

Maintaining a broader perspective will make difficult processes more bearable.

- These additional questions can help you keep things in perspective: "How does my discomfort now compare with the experience of the least privileged?" "What useful things can I learn from this experience?" "How is this improving my character?" "Am I able to choose how I feel?" "What options for action do I have?" "What would Jesus do if presented with this challenge?"

- Do not compare yourself to others who seem to possess higher achievements, greater fortune, or better health. Your view of their reality is incomplete and, therefore, inaccurate. Yet it can lead to discouragement. You are unique; you have your own particular strengths and weaknesses.

- Avoid catastrophic thinking, which is negatively exaggerating life events. For example, your husband has not called to tell you that he arrived safely, and you become fearful that he had a terrible accident. Or your doctor orders a further test, and you start thinking about a very serious or terminal disease. You do not have any evidence for such conclusions, and this kind of thinking will not contribute to resilience.

- Examine your past, particularly those things that were resolved but seemed tragic while they were occurring. These past events will help you see how much God cared then and how He cares for you now and will in the future.

- Remember that troubles will not last. The Bible confirms: "For our light and momentary troubles are achieving for us an eternal glory that far outweighs them all. So we fix our eyes not on what is seen, but on what is unseen, since what is seen is temporary, but what is unseen is eternal" (2 Corinthians 4:17, 18).

- Consider difficulties as opportunities to learn and grow. Do not allow yourself to be carried along by your first emotional reaction (such as frustration, despair, blame, or discouragement). Instead, stop the cascade of negative thoughts and say a prayer: "This is a hard time, Lord. Please turn this challenge into an opportunity to learn, and grant me the strength to face it with hope. Develop my character through this trial."

Resilience

- Talk to others. A trusted friend, a pastor, or a counselor could help you identify other perspectives. You will find that just sharing your experience with someone who listens caringly will not only lighten your burden but also help you think more clearly.

- Identify Bible gems to find solace in difficult times. For example,

> Trust in the LORD with all your heart
>> and lean not on your own understanding;
> in all your ways submit to him,
>> and he will make your paths straight (Proverbs 3:5, 6)

or

> The righteous cry out, and the LORD hears them;
>> he delivers them from all their troubles.
> The LORD is close to the brokenhearted
>> and saves those who are crushed in spirit (Psalm 34:17, 18).

Memorize these promises or write them down and carry them with you to read often.

Barriers, difficulties, and adversity have accompanied human history since the Fall, and they will continue until Jesus returns. Learning to live through them with the right attitude can draw us closer and closer to God. The presence of God in our lives is what makes a difference. For the believer, temporary pain may lead to a sense of victory, strengthen unity with the Lord, and build stronger character or resilience. This is one of the most precious promises contained in Scripture:

> The LORD makes firm the steps
>> of the one who delights in him;
> though he may stumble, he will not fall,
>> for the LORD upholds him with his hand (Psalm 37:23, 24).

Nine Habits of Healthy Christians

Reflection questions and activities for individuals

1. Create a list of Bible verses that communicate encouragement to you. Memorize a few and repeat them at different times, savoring their meaning.

2. Faith in God and hope for the future are two pillars for resilience. List practical ways that will help you strengthen your faith and maintain hope.

3. Are you naturally social and talkative? Or are you quiet and reflective, preferring solitude? What are some ways an extroverted person can be of service to others? And what about an introverted person?

4. Identify automatic thoughts that tend to overwhelm you when you are facing stressful situations (like when others lack punctuality or you are denied a request). Are these thoughts logical and reasonable? What are better patterns of thinking? What is their value when looking at them in perspective?

Resilience

5. What are the simple activities in your life that can help you through a storm? Do not limit yourself to religious items but also include secular strategies that are in harmony with your principles.

_____

_____

_____

_____

Discussion questions and activities for small groups

1. Share with your group one occasion when you struggled and bounced back as a stronger person. Explain how God guided your experience.

2. Read aloud the story of a resilient character from the Bible; for example, the story of Joseph in Genesis 37 and 39–41. Work together to identify the traits and attitudes that led him to be resilient. How can you apply his experience in your life?

3. Exchange with your friends specific positive things that you do when facing negative emotions such as fear, sadness, loneliness, or anger.

4. Maintaining a hopeful outlook may make all the difference when moving from problems to resilience. Share with your group what works for you when you must hold on to hope.

5. Identify a person in your surroundings who is going through significant difficulties. Discuss with your group various ways in which you can help that person, and then do at least one of them.

---

1. Ellen G. White, *Patriarchs and Prophets* (Nampa, ID: Pacific Press®, 2005), 472.
2. Özlem Ögtem-Young, "Faith Resilience: Everyday Experiences," *Societies* 8, no. 1 (February 2018): 10, https://doi.org/10.3390/soc8010010.

Serenity

Do not be anxious about anything.

—Philippians 4:6

Brian suffers from excessive and ongoing anxiety and worry. Things can quickly spiral into exaggerated reactions. He admits that it is not healthy, but he cannot control this tendency. He thinks too much about things that *might* happen and ruminates over the possible consequences of imagined misfortunes. In addition, he does not sleep well and is often nervous, irritable, tense, and unable to relax. This leads to run-ins with his family and coworkers. He may or may not meet the clinical criteria to be diagnosed with generalized anxiety disorder, but his symptoms cause much disruption in his life, and he is unhappy. He would like to handle his emotions better but does not know how. He is thinking about seeking counseling, but he is not sure. He must do something, however, because life has become too difficult, and he needs less fear and more serenity.

Anxiety is a major mental health concern. When we combine all anxiety-related disorders, anxiety becomes the most frequently occurring mental condition in the United States today—even above depression. Worldwide, after depression, anxiety-related disorders rank second. Issues of anxiety include disorders such as obsessive-compulsive, panic, post-traumatic stress, phobias (toward animals, people, objects, situations, and so on), and generalized anxiety (the most common type) with symptoms like those experienced by Brian.

In addition to the millions of people suffering from diagnosed anxiety, there are many who suffer though they are never diagnosed. The truth is that everyone may be subject to moments of fear, apprehension, and nervousness without an apparent reason. Anxiety disorders can be treated with psychotherapy and drugs, and the success rate is relatively high.

> **God does not want people to live in a world of fear but to experience serenity, which is the antidote to anxiety.**

While we should not ignore effective treatments that have been established through decades of research and professional experience, the power of the Word can be of great help in protecting people from these painful complications and alleviating the symptoms when they are already present. The Word of God acknowledges the universality and frequency of fear, as evidenced by the abundant use of words such as *fear* and *afraid*. But more often than not, we find that although people in Scripture experienced fear, the Lord reassured them, saying, "Do not be afraid."

Fear is one of the most powerful and detrimental emotions that people can experience. Often, believers feel guilt when they experience anxiety because they believe it signifies a lack of faith. But notice that God's response is to reassure, not condemn. God does not want people to live in a world of fear but to experience serenity, which is the antidote to anxiety. He encourages us to trust in His love expressed through His words of assurance in the Bible. The letter to the Philippians, particularly certain portions of chapter 4, provides counsel to aid the reader who experiences sadness, worry, or anxiety.

First how-to: Keep calm

We adopted our greyhound, Callie, at the age of three, the usual age when the dogs are retired from the tracks because they can no longer perform as required. Like many of these dogs, she came with emotional scars from her early life, which had been dedicated to extreme achievement. One of these scars is fear of riding in a vehicle, possibly caused by frequent collective transportation from track to track. As soon as the car engine turns on and the vehicle begins to move, she becomes anxious, with marked panting and pacing. She is quite capable of remaining calm except in this particular situation.

Serenity

One of the principles we learn from cases like this (both in animals and in people) is that anxiety is illogical and, in most cases, is elicited by stimuli that are harmless in themselves, like an engine sound or motion.

Anxiety in humans is well studied, and the goal of any treatment plan is to attain serenity. The most common type of anxiety is called generalized anxiety disorder, which entails excessive worry about certain things or persons: health, finances, children, spouse, misfortunes, safety, and even trivial things like household chores, being late for appointments, or the possibility of losing something. Another common type is social anxiety, where a person fears interacting with people or fears places where others may observe them or where they might be embarrassed. Yet another form of anxiety, found most frequently in children, is separation anxiety, consisting of excessive distress when separating from an attachment figure (such as their parent or caretaker) or place (such as their home). Phobias are also considered among anxiety disorders: incapacitating fear of heights, a certain animal or insect, going on a plane, medical procedures, the presence of blood, and others. Symptoms are very debilitating, and those affected often wish to control their emotions but have difficulty doing so. In these circumstances, they may find that they need professional help.

Many people experience levels of anxiety that would not be considered clinical, but they still feel afraid of a situation or of the future. This is normal and common, and it is then we can take comfort because Jesus gently reminds us, "Do not worry about tomorrow" (Matthew 6:34) and Paul adds: "Do not be anxious" (Philippians 4:6). Worry and anxiety touch everyone. God acknowledges this human condition and wishes hope and peace for us. We can choose to focus on Jesus' words rather than on what our imagination tells us *might* happen.

When anxiety, fear, or worry strike, Paul tells us to go to God, give Him thanks, and present our request.

Paul comforts his readers with shockingly simple advice: "Do not be anxious about anything" (Philippians 4:6). As with the advice to rejoice (verse 4), he is simply telling us "do" and "don't." You may ask, "But how?" The answer lies within the following verses—one of the most powerful messages in Scripture. When anxiety, fear, or worry strike, Paul tells us to go to God, give Him thanks, and present our request (verse 6). Please pay attention to the promise in the following verse. Nowhere does the text say that our petitions will be granted. There are other promises in the Bible that speak to that (e.g., Matthew 7:7, 8), but not this one. Instead, it promises that "the peace of God, which transcends all understanding, will guard your hearts and your minds in Christ Jesus" (Philippians 4:7).

This little passage teaches us a most important principle: the solution to anxiety is not to have our petition granted (at least not immediately) or to somehow garner enough faith but rather to freely receive the peace of God, one so great that it is beyond understanding. This means that when you feel anxious about your job situation and ask the Lord for a new job, He may not grant it quickly, or maybe, He will not grant it at all. Perhaps it is not the right request or the right job or time—but one thing He promises: He will give you peace and guard your heart and your mind in Christ Jesus. What a straightforward path to serenity!

Second how-to: Guard your mind

Cognitive behavioral therapy (CBT) is the most common form of psychological intervention today. It is based on the idea that changing the way you think will modify your feelings and your behavior. Take, for example, a young man who experiences worry and fear about possible life outcomes like, *I will never find a spouse.* He can be taught to reject those thoughts before they overwhelm him. Then he can be taught to replace those undesirable thoughts with more realistic ones such as, *I am growing every day, I have a good social network*, and *God will bring the right person at the right time.* Practicing this thought process daily would lead him to be at peace in the present and hopeful for the future. Following CBT principles, he may also engage in behaviors that might lead to a solution to his worry, like becoming active in projects that attract people of a similar mindset, which would make it more likely for him to meet someone.

If you have difficulty putting aside worry, we recommend the following strategies:

- Allocate a little daily time to worry. If you know that you have a designated time (it should be no more than fifteen to twenty minutes at the end of your day), it may be easier to postpone these thoughts during the rest of the day, which should be worry-free. During "worry time," review your worries (maybe list them), and see how relevant each is. You may worry as much as you want, but the time is limited only to the designated period. Some people report that pushing all the worries to a certain specified time makes it easier to review, and they discover that they even finish "worrying" before the end of the allocated time.

- Examine the logic of your worry. A logical analysis might reveal that your anxious thoughts are illogical. One type of illogical worry is all-or-nothing thoughts, such as *I must marry Gabriel or no one at all.* Another involves enlarging errors in logic: *They all saw me arriving late, so they will remember me forever.* We may also succumb to faulty reasoning based on feeling: *I feel afraid, so something awful is going to happen.* All of these thoughts lack logic and must be rejected.

- Ensure that your worry is solvable. Issues that are impossible to solve must be accepted and worry put aside. Jesus illustrated it this way: "Which of you by worrying can add one cubit [18 inches] to his stature?" (Matthew 6:27, NKJV). And for those things that are solvable, you need to establish a plan of action with prayer and reflection. This may sometimes require the help of a trusted friend.

- Learn to break the cycle. Worry and anxiety are, at times, difficult to escape because of their cyclic nature. They repeat over and over again, gaining momentum and placing themselves out of the person's control. If this is your case, you must have strategies to break the cycle: call a friend, go out in the fresh air, do a workout session, breathe deeply, listen to music, play an instrument, or repeat an encouraging Bible verse.

- Express your worries. Talk about your concerns with a close and trusted friend and listen to what your friend has to say. Some people find relief in putting those worries on paper so that they can quantify them, read them aloud, and then find a different perspective. This process is particularly helpful because writing and reading allow the mind time to process and gain a more realistic view.

Many CBT strategies, like the ones shown in the preceding list, have proven successful for the treatment of conditions such as anxiety, depression, post-traumatic stress, marital distress, or anger. But managing our thoughts goes much further and has enduring consequences. Back in the nineteenth century, Ellen G. White wrote: "If the thoughts are wrong the feelings will be wrong, and the thoughts and feelings combined make up the moral character."[1] Definitely, harnessing one's thoughts toward good goals is powerful and can result in desirable changes.

Undoubtedly, our thinking style influences the moral thread of our lives. For our own welfare, Paul admonishes us to harbor good thoughts: "Finally, brothers and sisters, whatever is true, whatever is noble, whatever is right, whatever is pure, whatever is lovely, whatever is admirable—if anything is excellent or praiseworthy—think about such things" (Philippians 4:8). He offers a list of adjectives portraying high moral standards and ideals. If you fill your mind with these, there will be little room for anything else. Without realizing it, such mental practice helps develop a better character, "for as he thinks in his heart, so is he" (Proverbs 23:7, NKJV).

Although sometimes thoughts are quick and automatic, much of our thinking is associated with our activity, good or bad. It is vital to carefully manage our activities and, therefore, our thoughts by seeking the true, pure, right, holy, friendly, proper, worthwhile, and praiseworthy. Guiding our thoughts into these things as recommended by the apostle can help us avoid worries and unnecessary obsessions.

Third how-to: Choose your environment

It is well known in behavioral science that the environmental context predisposes both mood and behavior. If you wish to leave worry and anxiety behind and attain serenity, seek a favorable setting. This includes the physical environment and, most importantly, the psychological environment (i.e., how you interpret and process the things of your surroundings). Of utmost importance is the social environment, and the Bible is rich in texts underscoring the effect of good or bad influence. Therefore, put the following into practice to achieve peace and calm:

- Place yourself in a peaceful surrounding. Treat your senses with pleasant stimuli as much as possible. Surrounding yourself with order, simplicity, pleasant sounds and sights, and comfortable temperature reduces worry or fear.

- Aim to think pleasant thoughts. Choose to think ennobling thoughts, not catastrophic themes. Ask yourself: "How else can I interpret this in positive terms? What are the real chances that the tragic events I imagine will actually occur?" Remember the times in the past that ended well and stop rehearsing those times that did not.

- Seek the right company. If you tend to have anxious thoughts and feelings, avoid friendships that increase emotional instability (see more in the next how-to).

Fourth how-to: Learn by example

Paul finishes his final exhortations to the Philippians by saying, "Whatever you have learned or received or heard from me, or seen in me—put it into practice. And the God of peace will be with you" (Philippians 4:9).

Our family lived in the Philippines for almost a decade. There, we learned that cutting a coconut quickly and precisely is a very complex task. It requires a combination of skills and strength that can serve to differentiate a capable individual from an unskilled one. In the past and in some remote areas today, a prospective husband could be chosen by testing this coconut-hulling skill. And how did young men reach the highest levels of performance? It had a lot to do with practice but also with whom they observed. Watching the "masters" in the community helped them sharpen their ability.

Observation and imitation are central to learning, and that is why the apostle admonishes the Philippians to put into practice whatever they *learned, received, heard,* or *saw* in him. Note that he includes all possible avenues of perception to ensure that learning, internalization, and imitation occur. Learning experts call this method observational learning or modeling. It is a powerful learning tool used in industries, schools, hospitals, and camps. One can learn well by observing good models. This is

> Watch and choose company that will help you be less anxious and less worrisome.

true in many areas, from instrumental and vocal music skills to medical procedures. It is particularly effective in learning routines of physical therapy, vocalizations, academic skills, cooking, sports, mechanics, public speaking, and even in the treatment of children with special needs, to mention a few.

Serenity is enhanced by observing and imitating others. Watch and choose company that will help you be less anxious and less worrisome. As you choose, listen to your friends' statements. If they are generally content, confident, and hopeful, stay with them, listen to their words, and imitate their nonverbals. But if they are gloomy and negative about the future, limit the time you spend with them.

On the other hand, if you do not suffer from anxiety but have a friend who struggles with it, sympathize with them, express your concern for them, and involve them in activities and tasks that distract them from those feelings. And if you notice that the problem persists and interferes with normal life, encourage them to seek professional support and help them search for it.

Observational learning also applies to moral (and immoral) behavior and may have eternal consequences. It is comparatively easy to be fair, generous, caring, thoughtful, humble, and of service to others when we have good role models. But it is risky to be surrounded by those displaying wicked, selfish, dishonest, vengeful, cruel, and greedy acts. It is also important to remember that each one of us is an example to others who are watching us. Inspired by Paul's advice to imitate good behavior, you may develop good character traits and actions. Try the following suggestions:

- Seek the company of people who have integrity. Observe others in your environment, and get close to those of good character. The Bible is rich in this line of advice (Psalms 1:1; 26:4; Proverbs 13:20; 14:7; 22:24; 1 Corinthians 5:11; 15:33; 2 Corinthians 6:14).

- Be critical of advertisements. Commercials are founded on the principles of observational learning. Attractive and happy people display behavior designed for the observer to imitate. Analyze the behavior displayed and ask yourself whether the message has any meaning or relevance to you.

Serenity

- Set a good example. You are not only an observer of others' behavior but a performer of your own. Whether you notice it or not, your life is partly public, and there are many people who witness your actions. You might help others or hinder them by the message you portray.

- Contemplate Jesus. Read attentively, think about the episodes from His life, and consider how to apply the stories to your life. When confronted with dilemmas, ask yourself, "What would Jesus do in a scenario like this?"

Reflection questions and activities for individuals

1. Do you have fearful thoughts or common worries? List them, think about their logic (or lack thereof), and pray to God with the list in your hand.

2. Search in your Bible for the experience of one or two of the following characters: Noah, Job, Moses, Ruth, David, Elijah, and Paul. Notice how they faced the uncertainties of the future, and ask yourself how you can imitate their example in your contemporary lifestyle in order to enjoy serenity.

3. When you feel anxious, how do you help yourself become calm and serene?

4. Observe and question others' behavior. As you see people engaged in various behaviors, ask yourself, "Is this in accordance with God's principles?" and, "Will I be a better child of God if I do the same?" Remember that just because something is very commonly practiced does not make it good.

_____

_____

_____

_____

5. What are the thoughts, events, or settings that make you anxious about the unknown? What logical analysis can you use to stop the anxiety-producing thought process? How might prayer and communion with God help?

_____

_____

_____

_____

_____

6. What are your "favorite" worries? Are they important or trivial? Real or imaginary? What circumstances trigger them? What can you do to break the pattern?

_____

_____

_____

_____

_____

Discussion questions and activities for small groups

1. Share with your group what the Serenity Prayer means to you: "God grant me the serenity to accept the things I cannot change; courage to change the things I can; and wisdom to know the difference." Do you have a personal example to illustrate your reflection?

Serenity

2. Ask this question around your group: When feeling anxious, how do you help yourself become calm and serene? Listen very carefully to learn from others' experiences.

3. Choose two or three instances where God, Jesus, or an angel said, "Do not fear." What were the circumstances? How do they resemble current situations in your life?

4. Let everyone in the group share one or two of their worries. Which ones are real and deserve attention? Which ones are not worth considering? How might verses such as Philippians 4:6, 7, and Matthew 6:31–34 address such worries?

5. Discuss with your group how people you admire can be an inspiration in your life, particularly in dealing with fear and anxiety. How can people adopt similar attitudes and behaviors?

6. Discuss with your group how everyone's behavior can be an inspiration or a hindrance to those observing it. Pray together for ways that you can be the "salt of the earth" (Matthew 5:13), particularly when facing fearful situations and looking toward the future.

---

1. Ellen G. White, *Testimonies for the Church*, vol. 5 (Nampa, ID: Pacific Press®, 1948), 310.

Humility

Do nothing out of selfish ambition or vain conceit.
Rather, in humility value others above yourselves.

—Philippians 2:3

Barbara and Beth are two supervisors working in the same company. Both have ample training and experience in supervisory roles. They consistently obtain good outcomes in their tasks, but Beth's employees are more satisfied than those under Barbara. Much of this difference has to do with the supervisor's attitude. While Barbara has an air of self-sufficiency, pride, and arrogance, Beth displays a quiet, self-composed spirit. Many organizations today are realizing that a humble boss is better than a haughty one. This is probably why the concept of servant leadership is emphasized to a much greater extent now than it was in the past.

A servant leader is a good listener, empathetic, and consistently open and willing to value others' ideas. This leader is ready to help and is committed to others' growth. With teams, she is trusting and a community builder. In the corporate environment, this style is often preferred, not only because it is being guided by high-order principles and values but also because it contributes to good morale and higher productivity.

One example is shown in the study conducted by Elizabeth Krumrei-Mancuso,[1] professor of psychology at Pepperdine University. She followed up on the leadership style of twenty-nine young people involved in the residence life program of a Christian college. These participants were new in their role and had to face challenges where they could opt for an autocratic style or a servant leadership style. The researcher administered measures to assess several characteristics, such as empathy, humility (both interpersonal and intellectual), and kindness to subordinates. The behavior of each leader was followed up for six weeks. Then, Krumrei-Mancuso assessed the features of servant leadership (particularly their use of power in the service of others, and not as a means to achieve personal ambition) as they related to subordinates. Information was gathered not only through self-reporting but also by subordinate-reporting. Results revealed that those with a greater degree of humility (being humble in both theory and practice) used more elements of servant leadership than those in the lower categories of humility. In other words, a humble attitude was, to a large extent, responsible for quality servant leadership.

What does it mean to be humble for the rest of us who may not be in leadership roles? From the apostle's statement, we can infer how it should inform the way we live: "In humility value others above yourselves" (Philippians 2:3). Indeed, a man or woman who values others above self is likely to be a humble individual free from arrogance, open to admitting fault, and ready to rectify his or her wrongs. This attitude smooths interpersonal interactions and brings glory to God, for it is in full harmony with Jesus' life and teachings.

Elsewhere in the Bible, humility is presented as one of the most precious virtues. The psalmist tells us that the Lord "crowns the humble with victory" (Psalm 149:4).

> **A man or woman who values others above self is likely to be a humble individual free from arrogance, open to admitting fault, and ready to rectify his or her wrongs.**

The book of Proverbs says that "before a downfall the heart is haughty, but humility comes before honor" (Proverbs 18:12) and that "with humility comes wisdom" (Proverbs 11:2). Paul wrote to the Ephesians, "Be completely humble and gentle; be patient, bearing with one another in love" (Ephesians 4:2) and to the church in Rome, "Do not be proud, but be willing to associate with people of low position. Do not be conceited" (Romans 12:16). Jesus Himself exemplified supreme humility in His life, warning His followers that "all those who exalt themselves will be humbled, and those who humble themselves will be exalted" (Luke 14:11).

Humility

Ellen G. White tells us that the Pharisees rejected Jesus because of His humbleness: "His wonderful acts of healing were performed in as quiet a manner as possible, although He could not restrain the enthusiasm of those who were the recipients of His great blessings. Humility and meekness characterized His life. And it was because of His lowly walk and unassuming manners, which were in such marked contrast to their own, that the Pharisees would not accept Him."[2]

There are also misconceptions about humility. Humility does not mean self-blaming, it does not mean denying what one is or does, and it does not mean keeping one's ideas to oneself, believing that they are not worthy. It certainly is not letting others push you around and walk all over you. A humble person may also be highly capable, assertive, and successful.

To cultivate the habit of humility, consider the how-tos listed in the following paragraphs.

First how-to: Know yourself

"Self-knowledge leads to humility and to trust in God."[3] An honest look at yourself will reveal your strengths and weaknesses. You will do well to appreciate your good qualities, skills, and abilities and then acknowledge that they are gifts from your Creator. Even gifts attained by persistence and hard work come from God, who gave you the necessary drive to accomplish your goals. You also need to admit your weaknesses and sinful tendencies, for there is no one righteous (1 John 1:8; Romans 3:10). This is humbling. At the same time, it should remind you of the gift of salvation through Jesus Christ, which is both humbling and amazing.

To expand your self-knowledge, you need to review your own life in all its possible facets. Consider the following inventory of questions (to which you can add others):

- What are your reactions when under stress?

- What are your most valued principles, beliefs, ideas?

- Whom do you love the most?

- What are the things that typically worry you?

- Where do you find comfort and safety?

- What are the things you are most grateful for?

- How do you view your past? Mostly positively? Mostly negatively?

- What is most enjoyable about your work, studies, or occupation?

- Are you mainly an extrovert or an introvert?

- What do you experience when you must delay your deserved rewards?

- How patient or impatient are you?

- What are your strengths of character? And your weaknesses?

- What are your strengths and weaknesses in terms of skills and abilities?

- What things have you tried to achieve but failed?

- What are the things you like and dislike in yourself?

- What would you do if you had a significant amount of extra time?

You may want to write your answers for your private use and reflect on them. A complete picture of yourself will be a good, balanced, and humble picture. This exercise will not only enrich your life but also lead you to thank God for His gifts to you while guiding you to depend more on Him to supply your needs.

Second how-to: Be grateful, not boastful

Contemporary lifestyle demands self-endorsement. It has become routine at work and in social circles (especially in social networks) to overemphasize the flashy events of our lives in order to praise ourselves directly or indirectly. But the truth is that even in this day of display, boasting, and competition, a humble spirit attracts everyone. In fact, arrogance is a trait that repels people. To avoid this adverse and un-Christlike trend, consider these ideas:

- Focus on others. Set a goal to observe other people's style and accomplishments. Instead of quickly presenting your case or experience on the matter, keep asking questions focused on the other person. Offer honest praise without exaggerating. Give them the credit they deserve. Show interest in the circumstances surrounding them. Lastly, demonstrate that you care, offering help in whatever they may need.

- Admit your mistakes. Admitting your errors is a noble thing to do. It sends a message of genuineness and keeps you humble. Some people do this easily, while others find it more difficult. But admitting your fault can be practiced in prayer and submission to the Holy Spirit.

- Learn to take others' comments in a positive manner. It is easy to misinterpret what others say (or do) and arrive at wrong, negative conclusions. It is a much better practice to give people the benefit of the doubt. If you tend to be suspicious and negative about others, try to apply alternative interpretations, and do not take things personally. Instead, try to understand the reasons behind someone's words and behaviors, such as temperament, past experiences and limitations, and even a person's upbringing.

- Show respect and consideration. A Christian should always do this, and especially with those who are of lower or unknown rank. A true test of kindness is to show respect for those who can be of no possible service to us. To achieve this, display courtesy and politeness, listen attentively, manifest interest through nonverbals (look at the person intently, nod, display adequate facial expressions), and do not judge, demean, or patronize. And if you agree with the person, offer praise and demonstrate that their ideas are valuable, even putting these into practice when applicable.

- Ask questions rather than criticizing. If you believe something is offensive, do not react through criticism or by launching a counterattack. Rather, ask questions to clarify what the othe person means with their words or actions. A question is likely to prevent confrontation and not upset the opponent. It will also keep the channel of communication open and help build understanding.

- Practice the discipline of quiet confidence. This has much to do with self-respect and self-worth. Quietly confident people will attract the attention of others when they begin to talk because they do not need to raise their voice or display some attention-calling behavior. It is the secret of being knowledgeable in an unassuming way.

Having avoided being boastful, be grateful and express gratitude to others in words and actions. Also, be grateful to God, adding His blessing to your prayers and to your thoughts.

Third how-to: Focus on others

Talking about oneself is a barrier to humility. Instead, purpose to carry out a conversation from a position of listening and learning about the other person, remaining open to their feedback. In so doing, you will obtain several benefits: a sense of well-being, better relationships, and improved physical health. You may also try the following strategies:

- Make showing interest in others part of your schedule. If you leave opportunities to circumstance, you may find yourself focusing exclusively on your own things. Instead, make it part of your daily or weekly schedule to attend to someone's needs or to interact with someone in ways where your focus remains on them.

- Use multiple modes: phone calls, texting, email, writing cards or letters, or visiting. Everyone has communication preferences. Try to adapt to others' preferences when you interact with them.

- Ask people how they are, but avoid the generic "How are you?" cliché. To do that, you should focus on specifics, touching issues connected to them: their health or needs, their children or parents, matters connected to their work or studies, or details about their future plans. Or simply ask them to talk about themselves, what Ida Cook in her book *Safe Passage* calls the "most flattering of all requests."[4]

- Be available often. Be the first to touch base with your friends. Contact them simply to ask how things are going with no specific business in mind.

Humility

- Suggest practical ways you can help. Listening to others' concerns is a great step ahead, and sometimes it is sufficient, but the next step is to offer assistance in practical ways to help solve existing problems.

- Avoid offering advice until you have a close and warm relationship with the person. Julian worked in Spain with American students who spent a year perfecting their Spanish language skills. The college there followed principles of simplicity in dress, and jewelry was not allowed on campus. As local instructors, we needed to alert students to this regulation, offering the rationale of our lifestyle tradition and the unacceptable image portrayed to fellow students and the community. We soon found out that telling them about the rule did not result in a change in behavior, or if the jewelry was removed, it was put back on immediately after leaving school property. However, if we first established a good personal rapport with them and then informed them of the rule, they were much more willing to conform and demonstrated a much better disposition.

- Pray for and with people. Praying on behalf of people does not require their consent. But praying with people (especially the unbeliever) does need their permission. When someone is going through turmoil in their lives, they seldom turn down an offer to have someone pray with them. When you pray for someone in their presence, it is a very powerful way to testify—you are demonstrating your faith on behalf of this person that God will bless them.

Fourth how-to: Grow in humility inspired in Scripture

Many Bible texts exalt humility and uphold the examples of humble men and women. Several Bible characters exemplify humility: Joseph, Ruth, David, Daniel, Paul, and many others. Jesus is the supreme example of humility through both His messages and His example. Another man, of whom the Bible says little but whom we know was humble, was Enoch.

The book of Genesis tells us that Enoch's father was Jared, that Enoch was sixty-five when he had his son Methuselah, that he walked with God for three hundred years, and that he had other sons and daughters. Most important and distinctive is that

"Enoch walked with God; and he was not, for God took him" (Genesis 5:24, NKJV). In the New Testament, he is presented as a man of faith who pleased God (Hebrews 11:5) and who prophesied about Jesus' second coming (Jude 14). Ellen White provides some additional details.[5] Enoch received visions about God's plans from the Flood all the way to Jesus' return. He also possessed very powerful intellectual capacity and extensive knowledge. These attributes, plus his close association with the Creator of the universe, could have given him a sense of superiority. Yet, "he was one of the humblest of men."[6]

Consider David, a humble shepherd boy who was anointed to be king. After having been blessed with much divine power, in humbleness, he went back to his sheep. "The great honor conferred upon David did not serve to elate him. Notwithstanding the high position which he was to occupy, he quietly continued his employment, content to await the development of the Lord's plans in His own time and way."[7] Toward the end of his life, David showed supreme humility when Absalom, after winning the trust of the people through pretended kindness, pronounced insurrection. Ellen G. White says, "The most eloquent psalm [Psalm 3] he ever sang was when he was climbing Mount Olivet, weeping and barefooted, yet humbled in spirit, unselfish and generous, submissive and resigned."[8]

Jesus Christ is our ultimate example of humility. Jesus "made Himself of no reputation, taking the form of a bondservant, and coming in the likeness of men. And being found in appearance as a man, He humbled Himself and became obedient to the point of death, even the death of the cross" (Philippians 2:7, 8, NKJV).

Reflection questions and activities for individuals

1. Take a few moments to think about how you relate with people—parents, children, spouse, neighbors, colleagues, superiors, subordinates. Are you humble with them? Can you improve certain relationships? Pray to God about this matter and place your needs in His hands.

Humility

2. Review your thoughts and behaviors over the past few days. Identify situations where you were boastful, humble, or neutral. What specific things would you have done differently, and what can you do to improve next time?

_____

_____

_____

_____

3. List three or four situations or circumstances that help you be more humble. List three or four situations that make it very difficult for you to be humble. What can you do to promote your first list and to change things in the second?

_____

_____

_____

_____

4. In a discreet way, approach a neighbor or acquaintance and show interest in their life. Disclose something of your own life and share how God has helped you. Remember that giving your testimony (or revealing your own experience) may move hearts more than plain preaching.

_____

_____

_____

_____

5. Choose one Bible character of renowned humility, like Joseph, David, or Daniel. Read the Bible records about the person and identify moments of humility. How do you transfer those moments of old to your particular situation here and now?

_____

_____

_____

6. Read Micah 6:8, which summarizes three things God requires of each one of us. Ponder how you can implement them today. Focusing on the third one, what are the consequences of "[walking] humbly with . . . God" for you and for those around you?

_____

_____

_____

_____

Discussion questions and activities for small groups

1. Why do you think that a humble style of authority tends to work better than an autocratic one? Discuss those reasons with your small group.

2. God has total authority over His creatures. How does He treat them? What would be the consequence of doing it differently?

3. Read aloud to your group Philippians 2:5–8. What is the definition of humility according to this passage? What aspects of these texts can help you become more humble in a Christlike manner? Share your thoughts around your group.

4. Discuss ways to practice "quiet confidence," wherein someone can attract the attention and respect of others without the need to raise their voice or use flashy presentation strategies.

5. Read together 1 Peter 5:1–11. What principles of humility can you extract from this message about relating to others and to God?

6. Ask each group member to share the traits they appreciate in others. Then review those traits and see which ones relate to a humble style. What is your conclusion?

Humility

1. Elizabeth J. Krumrei-Mancuso, "Humility in Servant Leadership Among Christian Student Leaders: A Longitudinal Pilot Study," *Journal of Psychology and Theology* 46, no. 4 (October 28, 2018): 253–267.

2. Ellen G. White, *The Sanctified Life* (Hagerstown, MD: Review and Herald®, 2006), 14.

3. Ellen G. White, *Counsels to Parents, Teachers, and Students* (Nampa, ID: Pacific Press®, 1943), 67.

4. Ida Cook, *Safe Passage* (Ontario, Canada: Harlequin Enterprises, 2008), 66.

5. Ellen G. White, *Patriarchs and Prophets* (Nampa, ID: Pacific Press®, 2005), 80–89.

6. White, *Patriarchs and Prophets*, 85.

7. White, *Patriarchs and Prophets*, 641.

8. Ellen G. White, *Conflict and Courage* (Hagerstown, MD: Review and Herald®, 2005), 181.

Positivity

Whatever is true, whatever is noble, whatever is right, whatever is pure,
whatever is lovely, whatever is admirable—if anything is
excellent or praiseworthy—think about such things.

—Philippians 4:8

Amy is in her thirties and lives with her mother. She works from home as a writer and is the prototype of a positive person—optimistic and, at the same time, in touch with reality. Amy is trusting yet not gullible. In her interpersonal relations, she is thoughtful and kind. When remembering things from the past, Amy feels satisfaction and acceptance. When she faces bitter experiences, like the serious illness of her mother in the past, Amy takes events as a challenge, and she does not generally harbor bitter thoughts but considers circumstances as natural learning experiences and a way to grow in resiliency. Amy has learned to enjoy the simple things of life, like walking outdoors with a friend or trying out a new recipe. And as for the future, she insists on always being hopeful and refuses to live in a world of fear.

Being a woman of faith, Amy finds great support in trusting God. She regularly applies Bible texts to her daily life, like using Jesus' words in Matthew 6:26 to say to herself: "[Amy], look at the birds of the air, for they neither sow nor reap nor gather into barns; yet your heavenly Father feeds them. Are you not of more value than they?" (NKJV). This strategy has helped her many times and has brought unspeakable peace to her soul.

The consequences of positivity are multiple. Most important, it helps people attain high levels of well-being and happiness. Besides, research shows that happy people maintain better interpersonal relations, are more likely to marry and stay married, do better at their jobs, are more successful leaders, enjoy better health, and live longer than their unhappy counterparts.

Negativity and pessimism, on the other hand, are quite detrimental. Those adhering to them will adjust their expectations to poor or negative outcomes and will tend to fulfill their negative "prophecy." They will also tend to suffer physically because of the tight link between negative thinking, negative emotions, and a weakened immune system. In terms of relationships, their mistrust and unfriendliness will not help their social interactions because others simply avoid negative people. In any team project, either at the workplace or in social situations, constant pessimistic comments

> **In this day, when depressive symptoms are so common, we cannot overlook the power of positive thinking, which counts among the best antidotes for depression.**

are likely to ruin the spirit of any group. Paul's admonition is very appropriate: "When you talk, don't say anything bad. But say the good things that people need—whatever will help them grow stronger. Then what you say will be a blessing to those who hear you" (Ephesians 4:29, ERV).

In this day, when depressive symptoms are so common, we cannot overlook the power of positive thinking, which counts among the best antidotes for depression. When Aaron Beck performed psychiatric rotations after having obtained his MD at the Yale School of Medicine, he noticed that many patients with clinical depression had the habit of harboring illogical and negative thoughts about themselves, the world, and their surroundings, including other people. As a result, he decided to help patients transform their mindset into something more edifying. This resulted in a significant reduction of depressive symptoms. The method was applied to other issues, such as substance use disorder, schizophrenia and other psychotic disorders, anxiety disorders, eating disorders, general stress, and even the prevention of criminal behaviors. This was the birth of cognitive behavioral therapy, one of the most widely used approaches to psychotherapy in the world today.

Positivity

Likewise, Martin Seligman observed that many mental disorders were rooted in people's pervasive and negative thoughts about events from the past, the present, or the future. In his effort to help people abandon their erroneous thinking style, Seligman launched positive psychology, one of the most influential branches of psychology today. As a result of these ideas, much of the therapeutic work of Beck's and Seligman's approaches is based on teaching patients how to build better thoughts in order to correct their inadequate thinking and overcome their disorders. As with pathological cases, the general public may benefit from these strategies to achieve more life satisfaction and prevent mental and emotional disorders.

Lastly, we need to be aware of the risks that accompany extreme and rigid positive thinking. The truth is that there are tragic and fundamentally bad situations in which we need not search for the "positives" but hope for something better. Furthermore, people with an overly positive attitude may not be able to assess danger and, thus, end up in difficult situations. Personal health is an example—it may be at risk due to excessive positivity when one refuses to seek medical attention or rejects important diagnostic tests with the excuse that "everything will be all right." This attitude also could be an obstacle to empathy: an extremely positive person trying to support someone emotionally may come through as insensitive and may end up dismissing important messages and feelings just because one "should never give in to negative emotions and should always focus on the positive."

With this word of caution, however, we must recognize that in the majority of cases, positive thinking is highly desirable. We should also recognize that each of us can make use of this kind of thinking more often. We will outline a number of suggestions in the following pages.

First how-to: Review your thoughts

In order to make your thoughts more positive, you need to look at the past, present, and future. Likewise, you should examine your thinking tendencies about yourself and about your environment (people, circumstances, physical context, and everything that happens out of yourself). Let's look at each in turn:

Nine Habits of Healthy Christians

- Think *rightly* about yourself. There is a classic concept in the field of education—the locus of control—that can help you judge yourself in a balanced way. Locus of control is made up of two types: internal and external. When a student does well on a test, she may utilize an internal locus of control and attribute the success to herself (she studied hard, completed all the assignments, listened carefully to the lessons), or she may attribute success to an external locus of control—in this case, external agents (the test was very easy, she got lucky, the teacher felt pity and gave her a good grade). Research shows that people of all ages who have an internal locus of control are more likely to succeed in many aspects of life. We'll mention one example. A British study tested more than seven thousand participants born in 1970 at several points in their lives. Researchers found that those with an internal locus of control at age ten were less overweight, healthier, and exhibited less psychological stress when they were adults compared with those with an external locus of control.[1] This is because those with an external locus of control believe themselves to be at the mercy of luck, circumstances, or the will of others instead of believing that they control the reins of their lives. Therefore, believe that you have the freedom of choice and the initiative to use all the gifts and abilities entrusted to you. This does not mean that you are conceited. In fact, for believers, internal control means that they have the choice (or control) to invite and accept their Lord into their lives and to live by faith and freedom in Jesus.

- Think in a *balanced way* about the world. Your environment, your circumstances, and the people you live and relate with must be processed in a balanced manner in your mind. An excellent lesson comes from Reinhold Niebuhr's Serenity Prayer:

> God, give us grace to accept with serenity the things that cannot
> be changed, courage to change the things that should be changed,
> and the wisdom to distinguish the one from the other.[2]

Positivity

This prayer applies particularly well as you think of your environment—all those things external to yourself. You cannot change the weather, your city regulations, or your neighbors' personalities, but your attitude and behavior can make a difference. There is no point in lamenting these fixed circumstances. Instead, you can put your effort into accepting and adapting to them. On the same note, there are many things that you can change, and this is where you should target your thoughts and effort. The serenity prayer fits our actions within God's role, which is to give us the wisdom to know the difference between what is and is not within our control, between what is possible and what is not.

- Exercise *insight* when considering the past. The past is one of those things that you cannot change. But you can change your attitude toward it. We all know people who continually lament that they grew up in a toxic environment, resulting in an unhappy childhood. Some attribute all their misfortunes as adults to those early life events. While it is true that early experience may cause trauma and adverse emotional consequences that linger for many years, it is also true that, more often than not, victims grow out of the adverse past and lead normal lives. Part of the secret is to put aside negative thoughts and resentment. Replace them with experiences that produce satisfaction and contentment; focus on accomplishments that bring about a healthy pride and serenity. Past blessings from God can definitely spur us on to push through difficulties now and face the future with confidence. As Ellen G. White wrote, "We have nothing to fear for the future, except as we shall forget the way the Lord has led us, and His teaching in our past history."[3]

- Think *actively* about the present. Truly, the present is the only thing that you materially have. Past and future are only in your head. A difficult past may lead to depression; a hopeless future may open the way to anxiety. The goal is to seek present emotions that bring present happiness, emotions like peace and joy. But the way you are affected by the past and present depends much on your thoughts and actions today. Paul presents our heavenly Father as a God of hope: "May the God of hope fill you with all joy and peace as you trust in him" (Romans 15:13). One of the greatest contributions of positive psychologist Mihaly Csikszentmihalyi is the notion of "flow" as the most desirable emotion for the present. Flow is experienced when we get involved so intensely and so passionately in a present task that we do not perceive the passing of time. This is the experience of artists, writers, or designers when they are engaged in their creative work. However, flow may be experienced by anyone carrying out any task, albeit simple, as long as commitment, concentration, and dedication are present. So, if you are developing a project for work, pursuing a leisure activity, or engaging in a social interaction, pour all of yourself into it, and you will be investing in positivity and mental and emotional health. Flow can especially be felt in a spiritual task—meditating on Scripture, praying, sharing spiritual insights with others, or volunteering to serve those in need. These activities will make you experience flow if done with passion and commitment.

- Think *hopefully* about the future. When we lived in the Philippines for almost a decade, we observed how humble people nearby survived adversity by looking to the future with hope. Every year, during the rainy season, typhoons arrived, and some of these tropical storms destroyed lives. Quite frequently, the torrential rains would destroy the meager dwellings of these families, leaving them homeless. After the storm had passed, we inquired about them or their relatives and learned that they had lost virtually all their possessions and did not have insurance. They would reply with a smile, "Tomorrow will be better." What a positive way to face catastrophe! They acknowledged that there was nothing good about what had happened, but they recognized that they still had the future, and they chose to look forward and to rebuild with hope and enthusiasm.

Once you have learned more about your emotional tendencies, you need to remember that you control how you think and feel, and then you can seek contentment, serenity, joy, calm, optimism, anticipation, hope, enthusiasm, and trust. In faith, you can hold on to this blessing sent by Paul to the church in Rome: "Now may the God of hope fill you with all joy and peace in believing, that you may abound in hope by the power of the Holy Spirit" (Romans 15:13, NKJV).

Positivity

Second how-to: Increase your positive thinking

Thinking style is the foundation of positivity. It is a choice: one can dwell in fatalistic, catastrophic, and negative themes or reject them to give way to affirming, elevating, and hopeful thoughts. The consequences are stated in the book of Proverbs in a simple and clear way: "A cheerful heart is good medicine, but a crushed spirit dries up the bones" (Proverbs 17:22).

Ellen White, in her book *Steps to Christ*, describes a letter she received while she was in Europe. It was from a sister who had focused too much on her failures and shortcomings and was writing for encouragement. On the following night, Ellen had a dream of herself in a garden accompanied by the garden's owner and by the sister who wrote the letter. Ellen was gathering flowers and enjoying their fragrance, but this sister kept mourning and grieving because the garden was full of thorns. The owner said to her: "Let the thorns alone, for they will only wound you. Gather the roses, the lilies, and the pinks."[4] The lesson Ellen White draws is that while there are always somber and discouraging events in the past and the present, we can also find sufficient bright and hopeful things for which to be grateful, and those should be the primary focus of our thoughts.

The following list includes tested ways to improve your ratio of positive thoughts:

- Practice self-talk. This is what Amy was doing when instructing herself: "Amy, look at the birds of the air, for they neither sow nor reap nor gather into barns." Apply this whenever you need a quiet reminder: don't talk, just listen (Psalm 46:10); look at the good side (Hebrews 12:2); be patient, the best is coming (Isaiah 64:4). In this way, you are giving yourself gentle and intimate reminders.

- Search for the good in things. The vast majority of situations carry both good and bad elements. Our minds automatically move in a negative direction, but you can stop that tendency and focus on the glass being half full rather than it being half empty.

- Avoid cognitive distortions. You may be pressed enough by stress to the point of regressing into thinking that is senseless, yet you may not realize it. In such times, a good friend may be able to point it out to you. But it is better if you can identify your cognitive distortions yourself and then correct them. Watch out for universal quantifiers, such as *always, never, everybody,* and *every time.* Watch for all-or-nothing thinking, such as when someone says, "Nothing I do will make any difference, so why bother?" Be careful not to enlarge errors and fears while minimizing good things: "I was late, and they will remember it forever." None of the preceding statements are likely to be true, yet one may take them as highly probable. This inevitably leads to unhappiness merely because of a wrong assumption.

- Avoid rumination. Do not preoccupy your mind with worry about a coming event or about something painful or embarrassing that happened in the past. Rumination is obsessional and repetitive and should be avoided.

Third how-to: Make it a habit

The goal of positive thinking is not to correct oneself once or twice and then go back to the old tendency. Rather, positivity must become a habit that is practiced naturally and without much thought. To cultivate this habit, try to follow these tips:

- Start with small steps. Choose a theme or issue where you tend to be negative. Find at least one positive aspect in it and think about it, repeating to yourself: "At least, I will get practice in . . ." Then, look for other good things, one step at a time. Once you've accomplished this topic, move on to other themes.

- Reframe your thinking. Reframing consists of looking at problems and challenges in a new, very different way from what you would normally do. Someone losing their job may experience depressive symptoms because of a great loss; alternatively, once the person is over the shock, he or she may look at the situation as a good opportunity to explore a new career or training or to strengthen ties with loved ones.

- Reserve a moment every day to practice the skill. At the end of the day, ask yourself, "What is the best thing that happened today?" Then recall one or two other pleasant or profitable events of the day. Get extra practice in using positive words to describe some good aspects of your life, such as *delightful, effective, beautiful, fabulous, appealing, thorough, marvelous, lovely, worthy, pleasant, powerful.* There are dozens upon dozens of positive adjectives in the English language.

- Practice gratitude. If you want to experience a positive attitude straightaway, make a quick inventory of the things, people, and circumstances for which you are grateful. This is a remarkable process that immediately enhances your mood and helps you see the bright side of life.

- Practice forgiveness. It has been consistently found that granting forgiveness brings about an optimal state of emotional and moral well-being. Jesus said, "For if you forgive men their trespasses, your heavenly Father will also forgive you. But if you do not forgive men their trespasses, neither will your Father forgive your trespasses" (Matthew 6:14, 15, NKJV). God does not refuse forgiveness out of retaliation, but the spirit you develop when you refuse to forgive separates you from God's spirit of forgiveness to the point of making you incapable of receiving it.

Fourth how-to: Lead an active life

A sedentary lifestyle has become prevalent today, and its effects are not only physical but also psychological. For that reason, steps to prevent mental illness and promote mental health almost always include physical activity. This is also true with positive thinking. Exercise neutralizes the effect of the stress hormones and favors the secretion of key feel-good mood hormones like endorphins, dopamine, and oxytocin. Physical activity will also distract your mind from focusing on worry or negative thoughts and will nurture a good mood in you and others.

Therefore, make physical activity a part of every single day of your life. Be sure that it is not an unpleasant experience. To make it enjoyable, follow these strategies:

- Choose a sport or active task that you like and persist until you have cemented the habit.

- Accompany it with music, a podcast, or an audiobook that may set your mood.

Nine Habits of Healthy Christians

- Do it with a friend to provide mutual support and motivation.

- If exercise for its own sake bores you, practice games such as tennis, soccer, basketball, or simply a vigorous activity with your family or friends.

- Introduce variety, such as new places, people, and activities.

- Choose the right level of difficulty; too much or too little may ruin your motivation.

- Focus on the well-being that you feel after an exercise session. Any discomfort during the effort will be compensated by feelings of accomplishment and lead to the habit of positivity.

Reflection questions and activities for individuals

1. Review significant events of your past. Which ones produce happy memories? Which are unpleasant? Dwell on the happy ones and pray for a better interpretation of the wrongs of the past and for a spirit of forgiveness.

   _____

   _____

   _____

   _____

2. What are the limitations of unrealistic positive interpretations? How would you help someone going through a trial that is overwhelmingly evil?

   _____

   _____

   _____

   _____

3. What are the small things in your life that make you satisfied and joyful?

   _____

   _____

   _____

Positivity

_____

4. In light of the Serenity Prayer, look at the past few days and reflect on the things you could change as well as those things that were impossible to change. Ask God to help you see the difference in current and future life events.

_____

_____

_____

_____

5. The concept of flow includes the most fulfilling experiences of the here and now. How can you achieve flow through prayer, Bible reading and meditation, sharing your faith, or reaching out to those in need?

_____

_____

_____

_____

6. Consider the message of Ecclesiastes 2:26, "To the person who pleases him, God gives wisdom, knowledge and happiness." How can you apply this promise to your daily life?

_____

_____

_____

_____

Discussion questions and activities for small groups

1. Discuss with your friends why some people exhibit a strong tendency to be somber and pessimistic about themselves, their world, and their future. How might the presence of God in one's life make a difference?

2. Share with others the situations that help you assume a positive attitude. What

about those that tend toward pessimism? What are some things that can be done to improve your mood in connection with negative situations?

3. Mention Bible promises that will help you be more hopeful. Start with Psalm 119:81 and Jeremiah 29:11.

4. Discuss examples of adversities that are happening in your community or country at this time and how happiness and hope might still be achieved in these circumstances.

5. Share Bible texts that inspire positivity and well-being and explain why they do. Psalm 37:5, 6, and Revelation 11:15 are good starting verses.

6. Share how you plan to create the habit of positive thinking.

---

1. Catharine R. Gale, G. David Batty, and Ian J. Deary, "Locus of Control at Age 10 Years and Health Outcomes and Behaviors at Age 30 Years: The 1970 British Cohort Study," *Psychosomatic Medicine* 70, no. 4 (May 2008): 397–403, http://doi.org/10.1097/PSY.0b013e31816a719e.

2. Fred R. Shapiro, "Who Wrote the Serenity Prayer?" *Yale Alumni Magazine*, July/August 2008, http://archives.yalealumnimagazine.com/issues/2008_07/serenity.html.

3. Ellen G. White, *Last Day Events* (Nampa, ID: Pacific Press®, 1992), 72.

4. Ellen G. White, *Steps to Christ* (Washington, DC: Review and Herald®, 1977), 117.

Contentment

I have learned to be content whatever the circumstances. I know what it is to be in need, and I know what it is to have plenty. I have learned the secret of being content in any and every situation, whether well fed or hungry, whether living in plenty or in want.

—*Philippians 4:11, 12*

Sally was alerted by a friend that she was becoming too preoccupied with shopping and purchasing. Ordering online had become too quick, easy, and available. Besides, handling and shipping were "free," and orders would arrive in just twenty-four to forty-eight hours. As a result, anything Sally thought she needed, she would impulsively order without further consideration. In the past, the time between thinking about buying and going to the store allowed for some time to change her mind or find an alternate solution among the things she had at home. But with online shopping, Sally ordered items immediately and was instantly committed.

More than a habit, this became an obsession for Sally as she constantly thought about her orders and arrivals. She also experienced a form of withdrawal, meaning that when the internet connection was down or for some other reason she couldn't shop online, Sally became uneasy. Of course, the spending of money, time, and effort had become excessive, and she felt a growing lack of self-control—when Sally attempted to diminish or eliminate her online shopping, she just could not.

In simple terms, Sally was not focusing on the things she had; she focused on what she needed (or thought she needed). This imagined need stressed her, and Sally found relief by acquiring the goods.

Sally's case leans toward a pathology, but ordinary people may also lack contentment and have a need to acquire things, thus falling into consumerism and increasing their risk of becoming shopping addicts.

Those in favor of consumerism would argue that it helps strengthen the economy and that it creates employment and national prosperity. On the other hand, those against it say that the excessive use of goods exhausts the available resources, damages the environment, forces people to work more intensely to earn more purchasing power, and deprives people of time devoted to their loved ones because consuming takes a lot of time and effort: earning money, deciding on purchases, and buying, using, and maintaining the goods.

It is necessary to review our behavior and match it against our biblical principles to determine whether we are embracing materialism and losing altruistic and spiritual ideals and values. In doing this, let us remember that deciding on this matter is personal, and we are not to judge whether someone else's understanding of a simple lifestyle differs from ours. Paul's advice in Romans 2:1 is quite appropriate: "For at whatever point you judge another, you are condemning yourself, because you who pass judgment do the same things."

Judgment needs to be upon one's own behavior, particularly to ascertain one's own problem with greed—for Jesus is clear about the evil of greed (Luke 12:15). Greed is hard to explain with logic, for it lacks consistency. We desire something; but when we obtain it, we tend to experience a further need, which could make us unhappy if we do not satisfy that need. And, as is so often the case, once the new desire is met, unease takes over again, and we want more.

Psychologists equate this behavior to addiction because greed has features similar to addictions, whether chemical or behavioral. Greed is obsessive in that the person continually thinks about and plans for the particular satisfaction. Greed is compulsive, and actions toward the coveted goal are constantly repeated. Greed causes withdrawal symptoms when barriers impede the attainment of the goal, making the person uneasy and irritable. Greed develops tolerance as a small degree of satisfaction may not be enough after a while, and extra "doses" may be necessary. Greed is shameful, and the affected person hides it and lies about it. Lastly, like other addictions, greed causes loss of control and becomes very difficult to quit, and the person almost always needs external and supernatural help to overcome it.

Being content is so important that it deserves your concerted effort to attain the balance of having enough without being preoccupied about wishing for more. If you need to improve in this area of your life, try to apply the following strategies.

First how-to: Practice simplicity

Learn the value of living a simple life. In contemporary terms, this is referred to as minimalism. Living a minimalist lifestyle is an experience in freedom. The story is told that a wealthy and powerful monarch of a remote kingdom was not happy. "If I could only find the happiest man in my kingdom, I could ask him to let me wear his shirt, and maybe then I would be happy!" After searching the land, his servants found an immensely happy man, as reported by everyone in his community. They quickly went to meet him and offer to buy his shirt. "I cannot grant the king's request," he replied, "for I do not own a shirt."[1]

Contentment lies at the foundation of minimalism. It is a mindset that looks at lifestyle and concludes that limited but sufficient resources are more likely to lead to happiness than the excess of things. Having too much takes too much time, space, and security to keep and maintain, which in turn does not translate into greater happiness and may, in fact, lead to greater stress and anxiety. American architect Frank Lloyd Wright, one of the most influential figures in architecture and design of all time, apart from numerous public buildings and community plans, designed homes for very rich families. Based on his long experience with the opulent, he is attributed with saying, "Many wealthy people are little more than janitors of their possessions."

Greed is hard to explain with logic, for it lacks consistency.

A few steps toward adopting a simple and enjoyable lifestyle follow:

- Avoid credit as much as possible. While credit may be helpful at times, it should not be habitually used.

- Consider the environmental imprint of your disposed goods. Although we cannot be using 100 percent recyclable items, we can think twice about purchasing items that, once discarded, will take generations to disintegrate, causing pollution, deterioration, and disarray in the environment. As stewards of God's creation, we are not entitled to destroy the earth. In fact, the book of Revelation states categorically that the Lord God Almighty will destroy "those who destroy the earth" (Revelation 11:18).

- Be critical of advertising. Much of the information you receive (e.g., through the internet, TV, radio, and mail) is designed to coerce you into purchasing things or services. Before buying something that attracts your interest, ask yourself: "Are the messages as realistic as presented?" "Do I need it?" "Would I become interested in this item if I had never seen the ad?" "What is likely to happen to it in a month or a year?" "Is this purchase the best use of my money, or can I use my money better in a different way?"

- Discuss the rationale for your purchases with someone close to you. This is particularly true when buying something expensive. In your consideration, examine the reasons why it is necessary for you to have it and discuss the options, beginning with what would happen if you simply did not buy it. Consider alternatives that are less expensive yet suitable. If it is a replacement, think whether it is necessary or just fashionable.

- Before purchasing something, take a look at your existing possessions and see whether anything you already have can do the job.

- Review your values. It is important that you not contradict or compromise your principles and values. Therefore, ask yourself: "Does this purchase align with my highest values (selflessness, empathy, sacrifice, frugality, and so on)?" "Is this something that will help me better serve God and others?" "Does it follow a line of simplicity and avoid ostentation?"

Second how-to: Learn to be content

Contentment is not a natural state for most people, at least not in our contemporary

Contentment

lifestyle of abundance and instant gratification. We all need to learn this virtue. When we purchase something, we experience a sense of fulfillment, but only for a limited time. The desire for more or for additional items will arise, forming the next link in the chain of consumerism—an easy trap. However, it is possible to stop this cascade of consumerism and to be content with what one possesses.

Here are some tips if you want to increase your moments and levels of contentment:

- Focus on what you have (not on what you do not possess). If you make an inventory of all your material things and put your situation into perspective, you will probably conclude you are fortunate.

- Learn to savor simple things. A source of well-being and satisfaction may not be associated with expensive items and pastimes but in activities to which you already have access. Think of enjoyable and uncomplicated tasks like preparing a simple meal, chatting with an old friend, or taking a relaxing walk in the evening with your loved ones.

- When thinking of what you already possess, include relationships, such as family, friends, brothers and sisters in the faith, colleagues, associates—people count among our most precious blessings.

- Focus on who you *are* instead of what you *have*. It is sad to find someone who bases their worth exclusively on their temporal possessions. Think of your attributes: good character traits that are gifts from God, your skills and talents, your beliefs, your cherished principles and values, your hopes, your reputation.

- Do not compare yourself to others but look inside instead. Keeping up with your neighbor's consumer habits will not necessarily work for you, and it may even lead to envy. "And I saw that all toil and all achievement spring from one person's envy of another. This too is meaningless, a chasing after the wind" (Ecclesiastes 4:4).

Third how-to: Lighten your load of possessions

Most likely, you have your basic needs fully covered. In fact, you may have accumulated enough resources that you are able to share some of your things without jeopardizing your lifestyle. Give away things that are in good condition but that you hardly (or never) use. Share part of your money and time. You will realize that when life becomes less cluttered, it also becomes more satisfying, and the act of sharing leads to a greater sense of well-being.

- Share more with others. Giving of your belongings to others brings about a great reward, as asserted by Jesus' words, "It is more blessed to give than to receive" (Acts 20:35). It will help you focus on simple things and find joy and contentment in what you have. Giving good-quality things honors the recipient's dignity.

- Give when you are asked. You need to evaluate whether or not you choose to give to anyone who asks. Professional beggars aside, when someone asks for help, it is usually because they have exhausted other options under their control and have reached what they consider to be insurmountable barriers. Only then have they made the decision to ask for help. You may become God's instrument to fulfill the promise, "Ask and it will be given to you" (Matthew 7:7).

- Give of your time, skills, presence, listening, and words. Maybe your financial capability is tight, but you can give in other ways. Think of someone who is unable to run an errand. You may do it for them, thus solving their current problem. Or you can visit, make a phone call, or video-conference with someone who is lonely, thus providing the gift of your presence to listen to them and maybe offer a message of encouragement at the needed time.

- Pray for others. Intercessory prayer is a precious gift that benefits you as well as the person for whom you pray. Pray together with them and pray for them in private. In doing this, you will be following Jesus' example—He prayed for

Contentment

Simon Peter (Luke 22:32), He prayed for those crucifying Him (Luke 23:34), and He prayed for His disciples and those who would follow Him in ages to come (John 17).

Fourth how-to: Learn from the Bible

All throughout, the Bible promotes the virtue of being content with what one possesses. It admonishes against covetousness, greed, and worry about future needs and supplies. Explore the Bible stories and statements that focus on being content and satisfied. Here are some examples:

- Manna provides a good lesson for being happy with the portion of each day. Only on the sixth day of the week were the children of Israel asked to store enough for the following day, which was the Sabbath. Apart from distinguishing between the Sabbath and other days, the normal collection procedure required faith and trust in God for tomorrow and action against hoarding. These things were very important, for God's words indicated that this behavior would serve as a test to see whether people followed His directions (Exodus 16:4, 5).

- The Bible insists on the immorality of coveting—it is one of the Ten Commandments (Exodus 20:17). The author of Hebrews states, "Let your conduct be without covetousness; be content with such things as you have. For He Himself has said, 'I will never leave you nor forsake you' " (Hebrews 13:5, NKJV).

- Writing to Timothy, the apostle Paul offers good advice warning against greed as a temptation and a trap that leads to foolish and harmful desires that, in turn, cause ruin and distraction (1 Timothy 6:9). It pushes people away from faith to end up suffering "many griefs" (verse 10). To avoid such outcomes, the apostle summarizes his central proposition with his words, "Godliness with contentment is great gain" (verse 6, NKJV). He specifies that having "food and clothing" is sufficient to be content (verse 8). And he explains that avoiding the love of money, which is "a root of all kinds of evil" (verse 10), will set people up to attain "righteousness, godliness, faith, love, endurance and gentleness" (verse 11), all of which are precious, immaterial jewels worth more than any earthly possession.

- Jesus clearly admonished us not to worry about tomorrow: "Therefore I say to you, do not worry about your life" (Matthew 6:25, NKJV). Also, He counseled His followers, "Take heed and beware of covetousness, for one's life does not consist in the abundance of the things he possesses" (Luke 12:15, NKJV).

- Lastly, consider the study and memorization of passages such as, "He who trusts in his riches will fall, but the righteous will flourish like foliage" (Proverbs 11:28, NKJV); "He who is greedy for gain troubles his own house, but he who hates bribes will live" (Proverbs 15:27, NKJV); "A good name is to be chosen rather than great riches, loving favor rather than silver and gold" (Proverbs 22:1, NKJV); or "Do not overwork to be rich; because of your own understanding, cease" (Proverbs 23:4, NKJV). And always remember that God can and will, according to His wisdom and timing, grant you what you need and more. "Delight yourself also in the LORD, and He shall give you the desires of your heart" (Psalm 37:4, NKJV).

Reflection questions and activities for individuals

1. Make a short list of areas in your life that you consider a source of contentment. Rank them according to their alignment with your beliefs and values. Think of ways in which you can practice them more frequently.

_____

_____

_____

_____

_____

_____

Contentment

2. What are your personal character traits for which you are especially grateful? Offer a thanksgiving prayer for them, and ask God to guide you in how to use them even further.

_____

_____

_____

_____

_____

3. Review the ways you are already sharing your resources (material and immaterial) with others. List some additional ways to expand your sharing.

_____

_____

_____

_____

4. Says Paul's personal testimony: "For the sake of Christ, then, I am content with weaknesses, insults, hardships, persecutions, and calamities. For when I am weak, then I am strong" (2 Corinthians 12:10, ESV). What is the logic of this statement?

_____

_____

_____

_____

5. Read Job 36:11 and Proverbs 19:23. Reflect on the link between obedience to God and contentment.

_____

_____

_____

_____

6. Memorize and reflect on these brief Bible statements: "Godliness with contentment is great gain" (1 Timothy 6:6); "God will meet all your needs according to the riches of his glory in Christ Jesus" (Philippians 4:19); and "The greedy stir up conflict, but those who trust in the LORD will prosper" (Proverbs 28:25). How would living by these maxims change your thoughts and behaviors today?

_____

_____

_____

_____

Discussion questions and activities for small groups

1. What are a few simple things that you enjoy the most? Let everyone in your group share their lists with one another to promote the idea that uncomplicated things can be a source of contentment.

2. Together with your group, remember events in the life of Jesus that show His simple lifestyle. Share answers and discuss how Christ's habits could be followed today.

3. Discuss with your group the similarities between being addicted to a substance and being obsessed with accumulating money or material things.

4. Share an instance where an advertisement has enticed you to acquire an unnecessary item. Discuss how you can critically evaluate publicity and be aware of its sophisticated methods in order to figure out how to protect yourself from its influence.

5. Organize an outreach activity where your group collects new and quality used items and distributes them to people in need.

Contentment

6. Philippians 4 reveals how to become content, whatever the circumstances. The NIV says that Paul "learned *the secret* of being content in any and every situation, whether well fed or hungry, whether living in plenty or in want" (verse 12; emphasis added). Read this verse in its context and find out *the secret*.

1. Scottish folktale, "The Happy Man's Shirt," Chorale Tales, accessed September 22, 2020, http://www.choraltales.org/happy.

Kindness

*Not looking to your own interests but each
of you to the interests of the others.*

—Philippians 2:4

The story of sisters Louise and Ida Cook, common British young women who helped many Jewish people escape from Nazi Germany before the Second World War, is not well known, but it contains a beautiful example of how ordinary people can realize extraordinary feats through empathy and kindness. Three years apart, Louise and Ida had a happy childhood with their parents and brother in Sunderland, and then London, England. With the beginning of World War I, the family moved to Northumberland, where they managed to live happy lives as a family. Upon returning to the capital after the Great War, teens Louise and Ida entered employment and became typists in the civil service, where they earned humble wages. Because they lived with their parents and practiced thrift and self-sacrifice, they consistently saved up enough to be able to attend opera events at Covent Garden and even take occasional trips to continental Europe and to New York City in order to experience the opera in these cultural centers around the world.

After each performance, they would greet artists backstage. Eventually, they became friends with famous operatic singers like Amelita Galli-Curci, Rosa Ponselle, and Maria Callas and with conductor Clemens Krauss. These contacts and their general devotion to opera would open doors to their refugee work in subsequent years.

It was Krauss's wife, Viorica Ursuleac, one of the most talented sopranos of her time, who introduced German music lecturer Mitia Mayer-Lismann to the Cook sisters for a tour of London. Mitia, a Jewess herself, told them about the ferocious persecution that Jews in Germany and Austria were facing. At this time, the Nuremberg laws deprived all German Jews of owning anything, and many were being sent to concentration camps with scant chance of surviving.

Louise and Ida felt terrible and wanted to help in some way. They learned about a British system that permitted Jewish refugees from Germany to immigrate to the United States via England. This system allowed approved Jews to quickly leave Germany and remain in Britain for a few months (sometimes years) while permissions cleared. The caveat was that refugees needed to present sufficient money or a financial guarantor to demonstrate that they would not become a charge to national public funds. Needless to say, seeing the rapid rise of the Nazi regime, hundreds of thousands of Jews wanted to flee.

These two sisters seized the opportunity to help. They began finding sponsors to guarantee passages to England for refugees. However, very few willing British nationals were financially able to serve as guarantors for a child or a woman, let alone a family. So, they devised a plan that, albeit limited, garnered a good number of guarantors. They solicited "subscriptions" of small amounts of money or hospitality to cover a case. When they had enough, they went to a friend or relative to ask them to be guarantors with the understanding that the money and the hospitality had already been committed. The person only had to sign the documents.

They also devised another method—risky, but highly successful—of providing support for new refugees. Some Jewish families had no cash, but they had jewelry and furs that had been hidden during the Nazi raids. The owners were not allowed to sell or take valuables out of the country. So Louise and Ida decided to smuggle those pieces from Germany to England. Then, upon arrival, the refugee who owned the valuables could cash them out to help cover their needs. Between 1936 and 1939, the Cook sisters managed to smuggle out many valuables, particularly jewelry, on weekends. Each Friday evening, they boarded the

These two sisters seized the opportunity to help.

plane from Croydon, south of London, to Cologne, Germany. Arriving in the late evening, they traveled by train overnight to Munich, where they had breakfast the next morning and spent the day working on some of their cases—meeting with potential refugees and receiving their jewelry and furs—which they promptly put on themselves. On their return to Cologne on Saturday night or Sunday morning, they stopped by Frankfurt, where they had additional cases to review, and then continued their journey to Holland's border to catch a boat to Harwich. They arrived early Monday morning and proceeded to London by train in time to walk into their offices. This route allowed them to enter and exit Germany at different ports, thus avoiding being identified as women coming without jewelry and furs and leaving with them. If they had more jewelry than they could possibly put on themselves, they acted like naive spinsters, explaining that they always traveled with their jewelry as they could not possibly trust anyone to keep it in their absence.

> When they heard about the need, the Cook sisters decided against fancy dresses, travel, and luxurious cars in favor of rescuing Jewish refugees.

What did they interview potential refugees about? They sought to identify the most desperate cases, help them with their papers, and assess their suitability to be adopted as guaranteed refugees. They always attempted to help a complete family, for they believed that it was not good for a child, parent, or brother to leave their loved ones behind.

How did they pay their expenses? In 1935, Ida was offered the opportunity to write a romance novel. The publishers realized the sales potential of Ida's creative writing style and asked her to write serial after serial. The royalties were quite sizable by comparison to her clerical salary, and Ida quit her government work, while her sister remained at her post. Significant amounts of money were allocated to finance their travel expenses, to personally sponsor refugees, and even to purchase a flat in London to provide temporary accommodation to their refugees. Ida died in 1986, but between 1935 and 1985, she wrote 112 romance novels under the pen name of Mary Burchell. Her writing business began at the time they learned about the needs of Jewish families to escape Germany. When they heard about the need, the Cook sisters decided against fancy dresses, travel, and luxurious cars in favor of rescuing Jewish refugees. They sewed their own clothes and traveled third class.

All of Ida Cook's books were fiction except *We Followed Our Stars*, a record of her and Louise's memoirs, published in 1950 and reissued in 2008 under the title *Safe Passage*. The book is still in print and includes all the details of the multiple acts of kindness of these two Christian women who saved many Jewish lives.

Kindness is a highly esteemed virtue recognized by most religions. The Bible includes references to kindness both in statements of admonition and as stories of characters possessing the virtue. Jesus displayed kindness in all of His encounters with people. Together with love, joy, peace, forbearance, goodness, faithfulness, gentleness, and self-control, kindness is part of the fruit of the Spirit (Galatians 5:22, 23).

Kindness consists of noticing others' needs and providing the necessary care for them to experience a better and happier life. Like all virtues, kindness must be learned. Sometimes learning happens naturally, especially in childhood, through instruction and by observing kind people in action. Other times, lack of exposure or bad examples makes it more difficult for this habit to flourish. But in any case, choice, and especially the power of the Holy Spirit, will make up for any deficiency.

Currently, psychological research presents kindness as a very helpful interpersonal skill and a source of well-being, particularly to the giver. This is especially true in relationships such as marriage, where kindness emerges as a good predictor of a healthy relationship.

Sonja Lyubomirsky, professor of psychology at the University of California, Riverside, has coordinated research at the Positive Activities and Well-Being Laboratory to find out and promote factors that contribute to happiness. This and other centers have carried out experiments where groups were assigned the task of performing small acts of kindness (like washing dishes for someone else, donating blood, visiting a lonely person, or giving money, food, or toiletries to a homeless person) for a number of weeks. At the end of the period, participants were assessed for levels of happiness and compared with random individuals who had not been asked to do this. Observed results consistently showed that those asked to practice kindness were happier than the controls.

How might these results be explained? According to Lyubomirsky, when people are kind, they perceive others in a more positive and charitable manner and feel a desire to support them when they are in need. They also experience the satisfaction of having achieved something morally good, thus enjoying the action and avoiding the burden of guilt. At the same time, the helper's own problems and worries vanish while they are supporting others. In addition, one's self-perception is enhanced because of seeing oneself as more compassionate and helpful, which brings a sense of optimism, usefulness, and self-control. Lastly, being kind to others generally causes a positive reaction in those people who are helped. They then show appreciation toward the giver and a willingness to cooperate. This feedback from people is one of the main reasons why benefactors gain happiness.

Kindness consists of noticing others' needs and providing the necessary care for them to experience a better and happier life.

But above and beyond the benefits, being kind is the moral thing to do. That is why the apostle Paul instructs Timothy to "command those who are rich in this present world . . . to do good, to be rich in good deeds, and to be generous and willing to share" (1 Timothy 6:17, 18). Jesus sets an even higher standard when He commands, "Love your enemies and pray for those who persecute you" (Matthew 5:44). In fact, kindness is part of God's nature: "Blessed be the LORD, for He has shown me His marvelous kindness in a strong city" (Psalm 31:21, NKJV).

The rest of this chapter will examine a few ways that we might practice kindness.

First how-to: Improve your empathy

Empathy is the ability to recognize, convey, and, to a certain extent, experience the feelings and emotions someone else is going through. It is a necessary step to kindness and compassion. Therefore, anyone wishing to be kind must practice empathy. Empathy is particularly helpful in relationships, for in its presence, people feel heard and understood and ultimately experience optimal connection.

Empathy can be developed through awareness and practice. It is true that some individuals are more naturally inclined to feel someone else's pain more than others, but it is also certain that everyone can become better at being empathetic. If you want to grow in this area, consider the following suggestions:

- Listen carefully by focusing on the words and nonverbal cues of the other person.

- Be available for opportunities to be empathetic. Even a casual acquaintance may need to express some inner conflict or trouble, and you can be there to listen and relieve their pain.

- Observe empathetic people from your immediate environment, from contemporary society, from past history, and from the Bible. Study them and reflect on their behavior, asking God in prayer to make you more sensitive to others' needs, joys, and sufferings.

- Practice self-talk. Self-talk or self-instruction is about telling yourself how to think and behave. For example, when Lisa, a busy professional woman, is presented with the opportunity to spend some time with a friend who has lost her job, she reminds herself: *Lisa, do not think about your things now; just listen, and focus on what she is telling you.* This prevents Lisa from being distracted and prepares her for empathy.

The Bible urges everyone to practice empathy. This is the intention shown by Paul when he wrote, "Rejoice with those who rejoice; mourn with those who mourn" (Romans 12:15). Bible characters such as Ruth, Boaz, Joseph, Dorcas, and, of course, Jesus showed compassion, which is a term very similar to what today we understand as empathy.

Second how-to: Start small and keep growing

Playing a musical instrument, crafting and delivering a public speech, or diagnosing and overhauling an engine are highly complex activities. But performing a small act of kindness is simple and easy. It also entails far-reaching consequences. Jesus said: "Truly I tell you, anyone who gives you a cup of water in my name because you belong to the Messiah will certainly not lose their reward" (Mark 9:41). The smallest act of kindness will be rewarded when performed with the love of Jesus.

Kindness can become part of your everyday life if you make a concerted effort to do small kind acts, thus experiencing the corresponding joy. With practice, the habit will grow stronger and become part of your daily life. These are ways to try to attain that goal:

- Keep your eyes open for opportunities to be kind. Be attentive within your own social group to those in need. You do not have to search for grand projects—a member of your household, a neighbor, or a coworker can receive your kindness.

- Consider multiple ways to perform kindness. You can do this verbally by means of praise, thankfulness, or affirming statements—oral or written. You can also smile and show a warm attitude.

- Practice kindness through action: send a small gift or a letter, email, or message honestly complimenting someone who is overwhelmed by work or small children; offer to buy groceries or run errands for a neighbor in need; help an elderly person with cooking, cleaning, or garden work; show willingness to help someone who has been a victim of a storm or other natural disaster; bring a hot or cold drink to the mail carrier or delivery person when the weather is extreme; take flowers to health-care employees at a hospital or to an elderly person who has recently received bad news; collect stories about a loved one who has passed and send them to their bereaved family; recall an old favor you received and thank the giver retroactively; think of some strength or good deed of your colleagues' at work and write personalized notes of appreciation to them; compile a list of Bible texts to encourage someone; share a book you read and enjoyed; when driving, yield to another car even when you have the right-of-way; give a box of prepacked food or toiletries to a homeless person.

- Be present. Sometimes kindness of the highest quality consists of remaining physically side by side with a person who feels rejected, bereaved, or hopeless. There is no need to talk or do anything other than to be there for them.

- Do something for someone without expecting anything in return. This is a great exercise in altruism, and the results may be life-changing. As this advice, often attributed to Winston Churchill, counsels, "You make a living by what you get; you make a life by what you give."

- Take care of yourself. Laura McClelland[1] and her associates from Virginia Commonwealth University observed nurses at work and concluded through psychological testing that nurses who enjoyed a high level of personal well-being were better fit to be compassionate and received higher-than-average patient ratings. Unhappy people are not able to serve others well.

Third how-to: Grant more forgiveness

Amy Biehl, a graduate of Stanford University, won a Fulbright scholarship to serve in South Africa, supporting people of color after the apartheid. She was sent to the black township of Gugulethu. Shortly after she began to serve, she was stabbed and stoned by a mob of angry men who saw Amy, a white woman, as representing apartheid's institutionalized segregation and discrimination. She was twenty-six years old when she died. Her parents, Linda and Peter Biehl, went through grief, anger, and confusion. But when they traveled to townships in South Africa and listened to the story of the four assassins, they forgave them. As a result of these experiences, they created the Amy Foundation in memory of their deceased daughter. This organization today offers arts and sports events, youth seminars, and after-school programs throughout South Africa to promote peace, forgiveness, and understanding. Two of the four convicted men are now active workers at the Amy Foundation. All these good deeds were possible because Amy's parents chose the graciousness of forgiveness.

> **All these good deeds were possible because Amy's parents chose the graciousness of forgiveness.**

The benefits of forgiveness have been demonstrated empirically across numerous studies. One example is the research led by Professor Zipora Shechtman[2] from Haifa University, with 146 Arab students who lived in Israel and attended secondary public schools there. To see the effects of forgiveness, the researchers divided the participants

Kindness

into two groups. One group participated in the experiment, and the other served as the control group. The experimental group attended a twelve-session forgiveness training seminar. The control group remained in their social studies class with their regular teacher.

Those who participated in the forgiveness training followed the steps of REACH, a widely used therapeutic model to help people become more forgiving. It is not based merely on lectures but includes activities and role-playing. The training was conducted by seven female school counselors with extensive training and experience in this model. Participants recalled an offense, tried to understand the offender, and considered forgiveness. In this study, the target of forgiveness was not any individual person but the Jewish society.

The original word for *kindness* may also be translated as *mercy*, *faithfulness*, *goodness*, *grace*, *compassion*, or *loyalty*—all highly desirable, godly virtues.

It must be remembered that when victims forgive, they are not condoning the offensive act, nor are they adopting the position of losers. Instead, the emphasis is on kindness and generosity. They review the benefits (physical, psychological, and social) of forgiving, and at some point in the process, victims are invited to grant forgiveness and let go of anger and grudges.

Before and after the intervention, all participants were given a test to measure how the program had affected forgiveness. Youth who received forgiveness training reported greater levels of empathy and less aggression, desire for revenge, emotional avoidance, and hostility than the students who attended regular classes.

Yes, the practice of forgiveness makes people kinder and less prone to confrontation. It melts away prejudices and brings people closer together. But more than that, forgiveness is central to the Christian message, and it becomes essential: "Forgive, and you will be forgiven" (Luke 6:37), and, "If you forgive other people when they sin against you, your heavenly Father will also forgive you" (Matthew 6:14).

Nine Habits of Healthy Christians

Fourth how-to: Learn kindness from the Bible

Many Bible verses exalt the value of kindness and urge believers to be kind. Take, for example, Micah exhorting God's people "to do justice, and to love *kindness*, and to walk humbly with your God" (Micah 6:8, ESV; emphasis added). The original word for *kindness* may also be translated as *mercy, faithfulness, goodness, grace, compassion,* or *loyalty*—all highly desirable, godly virtues.

Zechariah records the Lord's rebuke for Judah's selfishness, saying, "Render true judgments, show kindness and mercy to one another" (Zechariah 7:9, ESV). King Solomon reveals that "a man who is kind benefits himself, but a cruel man hurts himself" (Proverbs 11:17, ESV). He also warns against materialism and assures that those who pursue "righteousness and kindness will find life, righteousness, and honor" (Proverbs 21:21, ESV). The apostle Paul invites his parishioners at various locations to "serve one another humbly in love" (Galatians 5:13), "carry each other's burdens" (Galatians 6:2), "do good to all people" (verse 10), "be kind and compassionate to one another" (Ephesians 4:32), and "clothe yourselves with compassion, kindness, humility, gentleness and patience" (Colossians 3:12). Jesus Himself called the merciful blessed (Matthew 5:7), He instructed us to do good to those who hate us (Luke 6:27), and He urged His followers to love one another (John 13:34). He demonstrated kindness every time He preached, healed, or interacted with people.

In fact, Jesus told the parable of the good Samaritan, the archetypical story of kindness, an event that, according to Ellen G. White, was an actual event and not an imaginary one.[3] A man was attacked by robbers and left badly injured. A priest saw him and passed by the victim. A Levite did the same, but the third passerby, a Samaritan, felt sorry for him, treated his wounds, transported him to an inn, stayed with him overnight, left two days' salary for his accommodation and care, and promised to pay any excess if necessary. "Go and do likewise," is Jesus' command (Luke 10:37).

We find other examples of kindness in the stories of other Bible characters. Rebekah showed extraordinary kindness when she offered water to Abraham's exhausted servant and to all of his camels (Genesis 24). Ruth showed kindness by following her mother-in-law and committing to staying with her until death (Ruth

Kindness

1). David searched for a descendant of the house of Saul in order to show kindness to Jonathan's memory, and he found Mephibosheth and honored him instead of taking revenge (2 Samuel 9). A wealthy woman in Shunem showed kindness to the prophet Elisha by building him a room in which to stay on his travels. In response, the prophet interceded with God on her behalf, and she had a son. When the child later died, Elisha raised him from the dead. This woman's story illustrates how kindness often results in further kindness. On other occasions, Elisha kindly provided health and abundant food to the sons of the prophets and others by God's miracles (see 2 Kings 4).

Read and reflect on these stories and others that illustrate kindness. You will feel inspired by the power of the Holy Spirit to do likewise and apply kindness in your own sphere of influence.

Reflection questions and activities for individuals

1. Using your concordance (physical or digital), search for terms like *kindness* or *compassion*. Study the verses and their context. Try to transfer the situation to your life today and examine your opportunities to be kind and compassionate.

2. List a number of things that facilitate listening. For example, you might list things like looking into someone's eyes, not interrupting, or asking questions about the other person's account of things. Next time you talk to someone, put these things into practice, and self-examine how you did after your conversation.

3. Can you remember someone who offended you in the past? Do you still hold grudges? Have you forgiven them? If not, consider forgiveness after reading and reflecting on Matthew 18:21, 22.

_____

_____

_____

_____

4. Find three events in the life of Jesus in which He practiced kindness. Think of ways you can follow His example, given your gifts and your particular circumstances.

_____

_____

_____

_____

5. How do you interpret Jesus' words "Anyone who gives you a cup of water in my name because you belong to the Messiah will certainly not lose their reward" (Mark 9:41) in current times?

_____

_____

_____

_____

6. Make a list of specific, simple ways you can be kind to others.

_____

_____

_____

_____

_____

_____

Kindness

Discussion questions and activities for small groups

1. Discuss with your small group a few reasons why kindness is beneficial not just for the receiver but also for the giver.

2. Read 2 Samuel 11 and 12. Exchange with your group possible explanations for David's apparent inability to empathize with Bathsheba's husband, while he was quite able to empathize with the poor man having nothing except one little ewe lamb as related in the prophet Nathan's story. Based on the story, consider what barriers may prevent someone from exercising empathy toward another.

3. Ask each group member to share a Bible character that exhibited kindness at least once. What were the consequences of their actions? What would have happened if they had opted for an unkind behavior?

4. Jesus stated that the second of the two great commandments is to love your neighbor as yourself (Matthew 22:39). Discuss the connections of this great commandment to the practice of kindness.

5. "To err is human; to forgive, divine," is a famous phrase from a poem by Alexander Pope. Discuss with your small group the meaning of forgiving as a divine principle. Pray together to ask God for the power to forgive.

6. Plan and carry out a group activity where you can reach people with an act of kindness.

1. Laura E. McClelland, Allison S. Gabriel, and Matthew J. DePuccio, "Compassion Practices, Nurse Well-Being, and Ambulatory Patient Experience Ratings," *Medical Care* 56, no. 1 (January 2018): 4–10, https://doi.org/ 10.1097/MLR.0000000000000834.

2. Zipora Shechtman, Nathaniel Wade, and Amal Khoury, "Effectiveness of a Forgiveness Program for Arab Israeli Adolescents in Israel: An Empirical Trial," *Peace and Conflict: Journal of Peace Psychology* 15, no. 4 (October 2009): 415–438, https://doi.org/10.1080%2F10781910903221194.

3. Ellen G. White, *The Desire of Ages* (Nampa, ID: Pacific Press®, 2005), 499.

Gratitude

By prayer and petition, with thanksgiving, *present your requests to God.*
—Philippians 4:6; emphasis added

Ivy attended a seminar about enhancing interpersonal relationships and well-being that her local church offered. There she learned a number of strategies that helped her greatly in her everyday life. Perhaps the most notable was the habit of *expressing* gratitude to God and to others. With some conscious practice, these habits became part of her language and demeanor as she related to others and as she prayed. As a result, she felt happier, more energetic, more sociable, and more capable of expressing positive emotions than she was in the past. She now felt protected against symptoms of loneliness, depression, anxiety, and envy. In her prayer life, she made a habit of thanking God for even the smallest things: finding something she misplaced in the house, having a particular kitchen tool, catching the bus on time, enjoying a good night's sleep, and savoring a new kind of food. She regularly thanked others for all kinds of things, purposefully looking at their faces and not only saying "Thanks" but also offering a specific reason why she was grateful to them.

Developing thankfulness is a discipline, a habit that is cultivated through practice and reflection. In a sense, it is a philosophy of life. One can exclusively focus on bothersome and irritating little things in life and grow bitter, or one can find the positive in events, albeit small, and feel privileged and thankful to God and others. It is a matter of choice and persistence.

Psychologists have studied the benefits of gratitude on a person's well-being. They have studied variables connected to satisfaction and a person's reported happiness. But this approach is not conclusive because results indicate only a link rather than causation. In other words, it could be that gratitude brings happiness or that naturally happy people tend to display thankfulness.

More recently, efforts have been made to study this connection experimentally by comparing participants taught to practice gratitude with people who had no instruction in order to observe whether the first group displayed notable differences. Using this method brings about more conclusive results. Dr. Robert A. Emmons,[1] an outstanding researcher from the University of California, Davis, pioneered research in the area of gratitude in which he studied the effect of gratitude on physical health and psychological well-being. Participants were divided up and assigned randomly to three conditions. Some were told to write a list of things for which they were thankful (the *gratitude* group). Others were instructed to write down irritants they had experienced (the *hassles* group). The remaining were asked to write events or circumstances that simply affected them in the past week (the *neutral* group).

Results showed that the *gratitude* group displayed a more positive outlook and were more optimistic about the upcoming week than the other participants. This group also reported fewer physical complaints and greater levels of physical exercise than those in the *hassles* or *neutral* groups. Many experiments like this have been replicated with similar results. Mental health professionals understand that focusing on blessings is a sure path to emotional well-being and good interpersonal relationships quite apart from other benign physical effects.

The *gratitude* group displayed a more positive outlook and were more optimistic about the upcoming week than the other participants.

There are multiple benefits to an attitude of gratitude. Sonja Lyubomirsky, a University of California expert in the area of happiness, identified at least eight positive effects of grateful thinking: it (1) promotes enjoyment in the simple things in life; (2) enhances self-esteem and self-worth; (3) helps the individual handle stress and trauma; (4) inspires moral behavior, particularly when the thanksgiving is toward God; (5)

nourishes relationships; (6) reduces envy and jealousy; (7) protects against negative emotions; and (8) encourages the individual not to take good things for granted.[2]

There are two types of inspiration for our gratitude. The first is related to things. The second ascribes thanks to God for the good things we experience. Being inspired toward gratitude by things can be beneficial to mental, physical, and spiritual health. We can experience gratitude for people (friends, family, neighbors, colleagues), or for circumstances (work, the places we live, tools that help us do our jobs better, a current good mood, current weather). But being thankful to God is of utmost importance. Everyone can find blessings in the past and present that are attributable to the origin of all good in the universe—our heavenly Father—and thanks and praise must be given to Him. Above all, even amid the pain that we at times endure, we can be thankful to God for Jesus Christ and His gift of salvation. Through faith in the most reliable source, Jesus, the Living Word, one can look to eternity, beyond the times of trouble, and to ultimate assurance.

Being thankful to God is of utmost importance.

To enhance an attitude of gratitude, we propose a few strategies. Try them and see how you may start to feel happier and more hopeful.

First how-to: Count your blessings

Says the popular melody:

> When upon life's billows you are tempest tossed,
> When you are discouraged, thinking all is lost,
> Count your many blessings, name them one by one,
> And it will surprise you what the Lord hath done.[3]

It is a common tendency to forget the ways we have been blessed in the past. That is why we need to make a concerted effort to focus on the positive. We can take simple actions to help us capture and focus on those things, past and present, that are positive, strong, helpful, and beneficial:

- Write down your blessings. Whether you keep a journal, have a special file on your phone or computer, or jot them down on paper, writing down your blessings solidifies your memory and allows for reviewing in the future, especially when things are not going well.

- Think about your blessings at random times. When you are waiting for something or have a pause at work, retrieve some of those positive events, and fill your mind with them for a few moments. This will prevent your imagination from being occupied with the nuisances of life.

- Review them before going to sleep. Spend a few minutes at the end of the day mentally reviewing the two or three best things of the day and thank God for each one. This will help you transition peacefully to sleep.

- Try to find reasons to be thankful even in adverse times. British clergyman and scholar Matthew Henry was once assaulted by thieves that took his money by force. That night he recorded in his diary: "Let me be thankful, first, because I was never robbed before; second, because although they took my purse, they did not take my life; third, because although they took my all, it was not much; and fourth, because it was I who was robbed, not I who robbed."[4] There are blessings in the midst of adverse situations, and you can grow in the habit of seeing meaning even amid chaos.

- Focus on the present moment. Although you may be feeling anxious, most here-and-now situations are painless. That is why focusing on the present tends to be a good way to be thankful, and while you are concentrating on the now-moment, you will be guarded against ruminating about the painful past and future worries.

- Offer a prayer of exclusive thanksgiving every day. As children, we tend to ask for things from our Father, but that does not promote gratitude. Instead, offer a prayer to thank God for a list of specific blessings. Do not just mention the blessings themselves but also state how each has changed or is changing your life for the better. You will discover that the more you pray in this way, the more blessings you will find.

Gratitude

Second how-to: Express it

Pastor John R. Ramsey, in *A 2nd Helping of Chicken Soup for the Soul*,[5] tells the story of a church pastor who received a rose boutonniere from a church member every week for him to wear during the sermon. This became a regular occurrence. One day, when the pastor was dismissing the congregation at the exit, a boy approached him and asked what he would do with the beautiful rose on his lapel. The parson hesitated a moment and, before he said anything, the boy added: "Because, sir, if you are going to throw it away, I would like to have it." The pastor smiled and began to unpin it, saying: "You may have it, but what are you going to do with it?" The boy said excitedly, "I'll give it to my grandma!" and explained that his parents had recently divorced and he was living with his grandmother. The boy was grateful to her for all her love and care for him and thought to thank her with the beautiful flower. The minister was so moved that he responded: "Not only this rose, but you may have the whole bouquet of flowers placed by the pulpit. Your grandmother deserves them all." To this, the boy replied: "Thank you, thank you, I am so happy that I asked for one flower and got a whole bunch instead!" This boy could have run toward the bouquet in excitement to pick up his gift, but he expressed his appreciation using clear and direct words toward his pastor. There is no doubt that he was especially blessed after communicating his thanks.

The New Testament also records a story of gratitude and the importance of declaring it. It is in Luke 17:11–18. Jesus was traveling to Jerusalem and found ten men with leprosy shouting, "Jesus, Master, have pity on us" (verse 13). He sent them to the priests, and they were cleansed as they went. Realizing the miracle, one of them, a Samaritan, returned to Jesus, threw himself at Jesus' feet, and thanked Him. "Jesus asked, "Were not all ten cleansed? Where are the other nine? Has no one returned to give praise to God except this foreigner?' " (verses 17, 18).

King David was very open about his thankfulness to God:

- "I will give thanks to you, Lord, with all my heart; I will tell of all your wonderful deeds" (Psalm 9:1).

- "I will praise God's name in song and glorify him with thanksgiving" (Psalm 69:30).

- "Enter his gates with thanksgiving and his courts with praise; give thanks to him and praise his name" (Psalm 100:4).

- "Give thanks to the LORD, for he is good; his love endures forever" (Psalm 107:1).

- "Open for me the gates of the righteous; I will enter and give thanks to the LORD" (Psalm 118:19).

Gratitude is also directed to others. This is what Paul urges the believers to do: "For this reason, ever since I heard about your faith in the Lord Jesus and your love for all God's people, I have not stopped giving thanks for you, remembering you in my prayers" (Ephesians 1:15, 16). And, "Therefore encourage one another and build each other up, just as in fact you are doing" (1 Thessalonians 5:11).

Try the following tips to express your gratitude in a more intentional manner:

- Utilize various avenues to express gratitude. Write them in a card or letter, send a text message or email, make a phone call and talk to the person, or pay a personal visit and express openly and graciously the reasons why you are grateful to them.

- Communicate your thanks through action. Behavior and attitude are great ways to express gratitude. Do a random act of kindness to demonstrate your gratitude to someone. Purchase a small gift or choose an item you cherish and offer it to the person. Perhaps you can offer your help by running an errand or doing something you are good at, like repairing something broken, cooking, watching children, or shopping for necessities.

- Thank God. In addition to expressing gratitude to others, make sure to include in your prayers specific appreciation for people, circumstances, and things—material and immaterial. Focus especially on individuals by name: your friends, family members, neighbors, and anyone with whom you do business. By doing this, you are following Paul's example, "I have not stopped giving thanks for you, remembering you in my prayers" (Ephesians 1:16).

Third how-to: Turn it into a habit

If you are like most people—tending to forget the blessings soon after having received them—you need to make a concerted effort to make gratitude part of your regular language, thinking, and behavior. To accomplish this, consider the following:

- Practice positive thinking—it is much easier to be thankful when you adopt a positive outlook. Observing the half-full (instead of the half-empty) glass will lead to a more adaptive and optimistic assessment of things and, therefore, to a more grateful style.

- Make gratitude a central part of your prayer life—every prayer, even those of petitions, should include thankfulness. Paul affirms: "Do not be anxious about anything, but in every situation, by prayer and petition, with thanksgiving, present your requests to God" (Philippians 4:6). Gratitude is presented as a prerequisite to approaching our God.

- State your thankfulness to others systematically, not as a routine but in an open and direct manner. Don't only say, "Thank you," but tell them specifically why you are thankful. Think of specific acts, words, or ideas you have noticed and appreciated.

- Focus on small things. You may not often find life-or-death events whose resolution leads you to intense thankfulness. However, tracing the moments of each day, looking at the present and the most recent past, can be a great source of gratitude. The joy of finding something you lost, having a warm sweater or a comfortable pair of shoes, the efficacy of a little tool to perform a task, the well-crafted sentence you just formed in your writing, the lack of congested traffic one morning, or the tasty piece of fruit you may be chewing.

Fourth how-to: Find meaning in your challenges

Many adversities in life can be looked at with thankfulness. Others, however, are too painful to make sense of, like the diagnosis of a debilitating disease or the premature loss of a loved one. Only God knows why He allows wheat and tares to grow together (Matthew 13:24–30) for so long, causing so much pain.

Although challenging situations do exist and will continue to be present in our lives, we can choose how we deal with them. Julian's bicycle buddy and colleague at the General Conference headquarters, Frank, tells of his experience in his book *Living for God.* His wife passed, and as a result of the loss, he ceased to notice the inspiring colors of autumn and other beautiful things in life. In fact, sadness made it difficult to notice any blessing. His aunt suggested that he spend a week writing ten things he was grateful for every day, and why. Although difficult at the beginning, it soon became quite doable for Frank, and he came up with a number of blessings. He even turned many into prayers of thanksgiving, like: "Thank you, Lord, for my eyes, because they allow me to see color and see the faces of people I love," or "Thank you, Lord, for my toothbrush, because it helps my mouth feel fresh and clean, which also helps give me confidence."[6] Frank began to enjoy the "hidden" blessings of his life and discovered that gratitude, like a muscle, becomes increasingly stronger as one exercises it.

In addition to the technique just described, try the following:

- Look at suffering in perspective. As you look at the past, review the blessings that painful experiences may have brought to you in the long term. Look at the future with hope, in the understanding that, when things are difficult, they can only get better. And never lose sight of the hope of Jesus' return, which announces the beginning of eternal life.

- Personalize, memorize, and repeat Bible verses such as, "[*I am*] hard pressed on every side, but not crushed" (2 Corinthians 4:8); "The testing of [*my*] faith produces perseverance" (James 1:3); "[*I*] know that in all things God works for the good of those who love him" (Romans 8:28); "The LORD will fight for [*me*]; [*I*] need only to be still" (Exodus 14:14); or "[God] comforts [*me*] in all

Gratitude

[*my*] troubles, so that [*I*] can comfort those in any trouble" (2 Corinthians 1:4).

- If there is something for which you are not grateful, ignore it for now, think of someone who needs help, and go and offer your help to them.

Ellen G. White states this principle in the following way:

If you are an invalid, instead of constantly wanting sympathy, seek to impart it. Let the burden of your own weakness and sorrow and pain be cast upon the compassionate Savior. . . . Express gratitude for the blessings you have; show appreciation for the attentions you receive. Keep the heart full of the precious promises of God, that you may bring forth from this treasure words that will be a comfort and strength to others. This will surround you with an atmosphere that will be helpful and uplifting. Let it be your aim to bless those around you, and you will find ways of being helpful, both to the members of your own family and to others.[7]

Reflection questions and activities for individuals

1. Make a quick list of things you are grateful for.

_____

_____

_____

_____

2. Think of a specific time period or event in the past that was not pleasant. Are there good things that came out of it? If so, offer a prayer of thanks to God for providing those blessings in spite of the negative event.

_____

_____

_____

_____

3. Search for a Bible verse that brings you a sense of gratitude. Memorize it (or write it on a piece of paper) so that you can repeat it to yourself at various times.

_____

_____

_____

_____

4. Think of someone who did something helpful for you or brought some blessings to your life. Do something specific today to express gratitude to that person.

_____

_____

_____

_____

5. Is there someone for whom you are not grateful? Do you need to extend forgiveness? Remember, forgiving does not mean that you agree with the wrongdoing. Is there anything positive you received from that person? If so, think about that whenever this person comes to mind.

_____

_____

_____

_____

6. At the end of the day today, review your activities of the day—your activities, conversations, interactions, thoughts, and feelings. Offer a prayer of thanksgiving for all and ask God to give you the understanding and strength to deal with whatever was not a blessing in your day.

_____

_____

_____

_____

Gratitude

Discussion questions and activities for small groups

1. Why is it better to be thankful than ungrateful? How does this connect to our relationships? Share with your friends one Bible text that points out the goodness of gratitude.

2. Read the story of the ten lepers healed by Jesus (Luke 17:11–19). What is the main lesson Jesus is teaching with this miracle? What are other lessons you can learn from the story?

3. Ask this question around your group: When you encounter a bitter, negative, and somber person who rarely shows appreciation to others, what is your natural reaction? How can you improve? Discuss the ideas presented.

4. Share with your small group some of the things people typically take for granted. What can we do to be consistently thankful to God and to others?

5. Ask each group member to share a Bible verse that may stimulate us to express gratitude or to have a grateful heart. Print out the list and share it with each group member.

6. Use a searchable Bible to count the times that words like *thanks, thankful, grateful, gratitude,* and *thanksgiving* appear. Assign each group member to search in a different version. Compare the findings and summarize the circumstances where these words appear.

1. Robert A. Emmons and Michael E. McCullough, "Counting Blessings Versus Burdens: An Experimental Investigation of Gratitude and Subjective Well-Being in Daily Life," *Journal of Personality and Social Psychology* 84, no. 2, (February 2003): 377–389, https://doi.org/10.1037/0022-3514.84.2.377.
2. Sonja Lyubomirsky, *The How of Happiness: A Scientific Approach to Getting the Life You Want* (New York: Penguin, 2007), 92–95.
3. Johnson Oatman, "Count Your Blessings," 1897, public domain.
4. Quoted by David C. Jarnes, "Editorial: How to Feel Thankful," *Ministry*, November 1985.
5. Jack Canfield and Mark Victor Hansen, *A 2nd Helping of Chicken Soup for the Soul* (Deerfield Beach, FL: Health Communications, 1995), 32, 33.
6. Frank Hasel, *Living for God* (Nampa, ID: Pacific Press®, 2020), 62.
7. Ellen G. White, *The Ministry of Health and Healing* (Nampa, ID: Pacific Press®, 2004), 142.